WATERFALL WALKS

TEESDALE & THE HIGH PENNINES

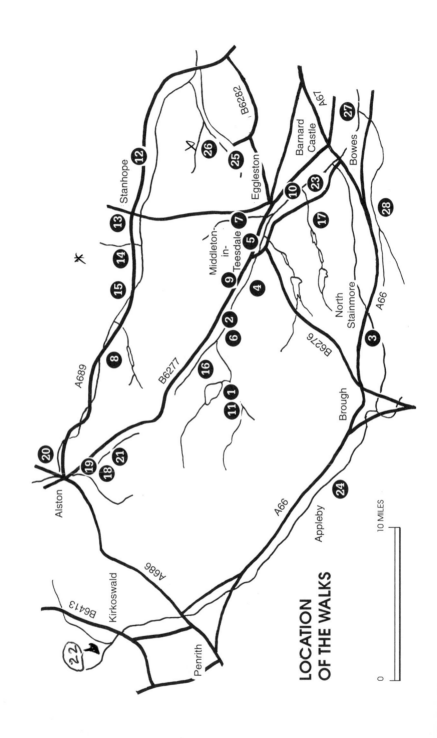

LOCATION
OF THE WALKS

0   10 MILES

WATERFALL WALKS
TEESDALE &
THE HIGH PENNINES

by

MARY WELSH

Illustrated by

LINDA WATERS

CICERONE PRESS
MILNTHORPE, CUMBRIA

WATERFALL WALKS - TEESDALE & HIGH PENNINES

© Mary Welsh

ISBN 1 85284 158 3

A catalogue record for this book is available from the British Library

ACKNOWLEDGEMENTS

My grateful thanks go to Maureen Fleming and Joan Morgan, who helped me research these walks, to my husband Tom, who gave me enormous support, to Linda Waters, whose illustrations must persuade all to seek out these hidden corners of Teesdale, and last to Cami, my now elderly border collie, who still plods on, loving Teesdale as much as I do.

ADVICE TO READERS

Readers are advised that whilst every effort is taken by the author to ensure the accuracy of this guidebook, changes can occur which may affect the contents. It is advisable to check locally on transport, accommodation, shops etc but even rights of way can be altered.

The publisher would welcome notes of any such changes.

CONTENTS

ring ouzel . . .
"its loud, clear song"(walk 5)

PREFACE

I t has been a great pleasure to devise these mainly circular walks, each of which has a waterfall as its focal point. I have taken the walker to the famous falls of Teesdale and the High Pennines, and also to many which, though less well known, are glorious to view.

The area is compelling walking country - wild and rough in winter but welcoming in spring as the migrating birds return and the woodlands become a mosaic of soft greens. In early summer the mountain pansies, spring gentians, primroses, bird's-eye primroses, cowslips and globe flowers of the hay meadows leave you breathless with their beauty. And in autumn the changing colours of the moors and trees entice you back again and again.

I have written walks throughout the year, recording the plants and animal life I have seen and hoping the walker will see too. I have visited waterfalls shown on the Teesdale map (OS Outdoor Leisure 31), and where a few stray off the edges I have given the number of the relevant Pathfinder map. For the actual waterfall I have given the grid reference.

The waterfall seen in the Nunnery walks is well off the Teesdale map, but it is a glorious walk with spectacular falls and I hope no one will object to its being added to this book.

Teesdale and the High Pennines can pass through the weather of the four seasons in a day. It is always advisable to go prepared for such eventualities, carrying waterproofs, extra food, compass, map and whistle and wearing strong footwear. Farmers work hard to earn a living in this beautiful area, so please observe requests to keep dogs under close control and keep to the rights of way.

Cauldron Snout

1. Cauldron Snout, Upper Teesdale

GR 814286, 8 miles

PARK AT the Wheelhead Sike car park on the edge of Cow Green Reservoir. From here walk back down Peghorn lane and enjoy the extensive views of Upper Teesdale. White about the slopes and limestone walls criss-cross the greening fells.

On either side of the lane lapwings court with erratic flight. Redshanks, also busy with their nuptials, rise trilling melodiously on quivering wings. And curlews utter their bubbling calls as they establish their territories.

Walk for 2¹/₂ miles along the lane to a cattle grid just beyond a whitewashed barn on the left. A well signposted farm track leads towards Widdy Bank Farm, Cauldron Snout and the Upper Teesdale Nature Reserve. Walk right along the track and enjoy the skylarks, singing as they rise above the moorland. A snipe, feeding quietly in an oozy flush beside a small stream, flies off rapidly.

Just before the farm is reached the track joins the Pennine Way - the second longest footpath in England. Pass through the outbuildings and stride on beside the River Tees, where dippers fly upstream. On the other side of the gently flowing water lie the forbidding slopes of Cronkley Fell. After 100yds the reinforced track ceases and an indistinct path continues over grassy Holmwath below Widdy Bank. And then the path lies over and through a confusion of tumbled boulders which provide easy scrambling in dry weather but require considerable care when wet. Above tower the steep slopes of the fell, where grow great banks of heather. A pair of grouse fly overhead to the far bank in search of succulent heather shoots, calling harshly as they go.

At Lingy Holm the path moves away from the riverside and well placed duckboards take the walker dry-shod across a wet area. Pause here and look for a multitude of frogs busy mating. Large clumps of spawn float at the surface of the sun-warmed pools.

Look upwards to the prominent crags of Falcon Clints, which are composed of six-sided blocks of Whin Sill rock. Continue over

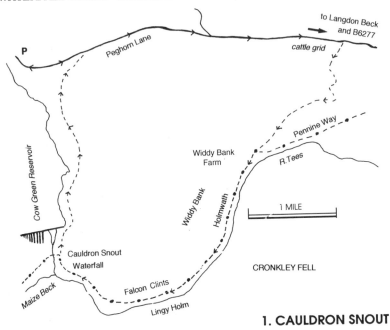

1. CAULDRON SNOUT

another easier boulder strewn area and pass into a part of the river valley where the steep slopes on either side give shelter from an occasional sharp gust of wind. To the right a narrow beck comes racing downwards to unite with the Tees. Ahead lies the confluence of the Maize Beck and the River Tees.

Follow the path as it abruptly turns north, and in front of you lies the great reward of the walk. Cauldron Snout descends in large foaming cascades for 200ft over the Great Whin Sill. The footpath, a long upward scramble, climbs beside the fine mountain torrent. Again take care as you go, especially if the rocks are wet.

The noise is tremendous as the huge mass of bronze streaked water roars through the imprisoning rock walls. At the top of the fall lies the huge Cow Green Dam and beyond stretch the peaceful waters of the reservoir.

Bear right onto the reinforced track to walk through the Widdybank Fell Nature Trail. Here, at various numbered stations, at the right time of the year, you may find mountain pansy, common rockrose, northern bedstraw, moonwort, yellow mountain

10

saxifrage, the Teesdale violet and other arctic and alpine plants.

After 1¹/₂ miles take a left fork along a track across the moorland. Then follow a narrow path off to the right that returns to the car park.

Mountain pansy

High Force

12

2. High Force, Upper Teesdale

GR 881286, 3¹/₂ miles

P ARK AT the popular picnic area and car park close to the High Force Hotel on the B6277 west of Middleton-in-Teesdale. Opposite the hotel, pay your admission money and stroll the splendid woodland walk. The reinforced way, wide enough for wheelchairs, slopes gently towards the Tees. It was rebuilt after a storm on the night of January 2 1992 devastated part of High Force Woods, through which it passes. Many of the trees destroyed were more than 100 years old and some were more than 100ft high.

The path winds round below a huge outcrops of sedimentary rock, high above the surging river. And then quite suddenly you have your first, and perhaps the most pleasing, view of the magnificent force.

Continue on and descend, with care, the stone steps to the edge of the boiling water. As this grand force drops 70ft into an amphitheatre of sheer-sided whin sill it fills the head of the gorge with a tremendous noise. Clouds of spray fly into the air and rainbows play over the fall. Be prepared for a drenching if you visit the force when the river is in spate. View with care and heed the warnings given on safety.

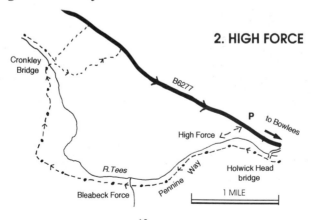

13

Return to the road and walk downhill for 50yds in the direction of Middleton-in-Teesdale. By the signs "No footway 600 yards" and "Public footpath" turn right to descend Crag Path, a well-constructed flight of steps towards the River Tees. Stroll the pleasing riverside path to Holwick Head Bridge, which you cross to join the Pennine Way. Turn right and climb the stepped path to a stile by a gate to enter the Upper Teesdale National Nature Reserve, where there is an instructive notice board.

Stride the reinforced path through a very large area of juniper loaded with purpling berries which much delight a host of coal tits. Follow the way to the edge of the unfenced whinstone cliffs and with care enjoy another view of dramatic High Force.

Beyond, the way, coming close to the hurrying Tees, leads over open fell. On the opposite bank lies the huge quarry from which whin sill is wrested for stone for bank vaults. To your left the graceful Bleabeck Force descends in a series of elegant cascades.

Walk on over Pasture Foot, where grouse feed on heathery slopes. They rise with noisy whirring wings as they fly just above the vegetation to safer feeding ground. Climb Bracken Rigg and look across the steep slopes of Dine Holm Scar. Pass through a stile in the right-hand corner of the wall ahead. Turn right to climb a slope on a series of duckboards, keeping the wall to your right. Then descend the slope to more duckboards, leading to a stile on the right. Beyond, turn left, cross even more duckboards and then head down a rock-strewn gully between huge banks of juniper.

At the bottom, pass through a gate on the left, with an acorn sign on the gate post. Beyond, turn right, keeping the wall to the right, and climb the slope to Cronkley Farm. Turn left beyond the farm gate and stride along the farm track to cross Cronkley Bridge. In winter fieldfare feed in the pastures, mingling with a flock of lapwing, and in early spring curlew fly overhead uttering their long, liquid, bubbling calls.

Continue along the farm track as it swings right and climbs the slope towards Hill End farm. Just before the cattle grid pass through the gate 25yds to the right. Walk ahead, following the waymark, with the wall to the left. Away to the right you can see White Force, visited on walk 6. Pass through the gate and follow the sunken track that continues ahead and then curves left with the wall, now to your right. Over the wall lie rough rock-strewn

Coal tit on juniper

slopes and here, in June, a pair of ring ouzels feed their large youngsters, who clamour continuously for food. Continue beyond the next waymarked gate and carry on with the wall still to your right. Join a farm track and walk right. Pass through the gate and continue. Here in a fenced meadow grows a magnificent carpet of mountain pansies.

Stride on past West Force Garth farm and East Force Garth farm and follow the farm access track to the tarmac road. Turn left and continue to where it forks. Take the right branch and then turn right along the B6277 to return to the car park.

Dowgill Beck

3. Dowgill Falls between North and South Stainmore

GRs 845141, 844139, 847146, (PF NY 81/91,
589 North Stainmore & Bowes) 4¹/₂ miles

L EAVE BROUGH by the A66 in an easterly direction. Just over a mile beyond North Stainmore, park in a wide layby on the far side of the road. Walk the cart-track that leads from the layby. Look for the small waterfall on your left and then take the first gate on your right. Follow the grassy track, deeply sunken in places, that drops downhill to Light Trees farm.

Walk to the right of the farm and notice the culverted tractor bridge over the Dowgill Beck. Do not cross but walk downstream, past the first of many glorious falls on this lovely beck, to a squeeze stile. Continue ahead beside the hurrying water. The beck is lined with ash trees whose pale bark gives its name to the farm. Pass through the next gated stile to walk beside a large meander. Just beyond, look for another charming fall.

3. DOWGILL FALLS

For a short distance a wall separates you from the beck. Use a gap stile in the wall to return to it. Cross the footbridge beyond and continue downstream. View another fall beneath ash trees and then another, just before a ford, again shadowed by ash. A few yards on, below the ford, white-topped water dancing over ledges of rock creates a lace-like cascade before raging on to descend in another elegant fall. Enjoy this grand show of petulance by the Dowgill Beck.

17

Pass through a gate on the right before Low Dowgill farm, where a ewe tends her new-born lambs. Walk to the right of the dwelling and pass through a gate adjoining the house. Stride ahead, dropping down a steep grassy slope to a tree-girt hollow. Pass through a gate and cross a plank over a narrow stream. Keep left beside the stream to a gate into a nature reserve.

From now on the walk becomes sheer magic. Follow the footpath through woodland to the side of the Dowgill Beck and walk downstream. Primroses, celandines and wood anemones line the way, a dipper flies low over the water and four roe deer bound up the side of the tree-lined gill. The path comes to the place where the Dowgill Beck joins the Argill Beck. The combined waters descend in a tempestuous fall stained with peat. Hazel trees lean over the water and each dangling, golden catkin catches the sunlight.

Continue downstream beside the Argill Beck, past more hazels laden with catkins and pussy willow aglow with yellow flowers, to a footbridge, which you cross. Strike uphill, bearing slightly to the right. There is no visible path so pick your way, avoiding hollows and some deeper depressions. Keep to the left of one very steep-sided hollow which runs down to the beck and then follow a short wall that leads to a rickety stile at the edge of a narrow stream. Step across and climb up the short slope ahead.

Across the pasture in front of you stands a stone barn and to the left, set among trees, is The Old Vicarage, now a farm. Follow the wall on your right to pass left of the barn and then continue to the farm. Pass between the buildings and walk the access track beyond. From the pastures around the farm come the continual calls of curlews as they establish their nest sites.

Where the track swings left, turn right to walk a metalled track to South Stainmore church and school. The tiny church with its belfry and white door stands serenely in this quiet corner of Cumbria.

Continue along the track to a narrow lane. Turn right and walk on. To the right there is a good view of Brough Castle. Beneath the hedgerow are red dead-nettle flowers. At Gillses farm, turn right onto a cart-track beyond two railway wagons used as farm buildings. Continue ahead, ignoring the left branch, to pass Lowfield. Walk on to Old Park. Look for the stile to the left of the house in the far left corner of the garden. Beyond, walk ahead across the pasture to a tied gate. Walk on ahead over a pasture and then drop down the wooded slope to a footbridge over the Ar gill Beck.

Once on the far side, turn right, climb a small slope an continue right through the trees, keeping the beck to your right. Look for the pretty pink "roses", male flowers, on the larch that overhang the way. The indistinct path comes to the side of a feeder str eam. Walk upstream for 100yds and step across. Look for the place where the top strand of barbed wire of the wire fence has been cut and bent back.

Beyond, turn left. The path keeps close to the fence on the left that runs along the edge of the very steep gill thr ough which the tiny stream hurries. Continue until the path comes level with the tiny stream and a small turf bank across the water. Climb the wire fence on the far side of the str eam - again the barbed wire top strand has been cut and folded back. Follow the footpath beyond that leads to a stile on the left side of Dike House. This stile has

Culverted bridge over Dowgill

two rows of barbed wire, but it also has a large boulder on either side to help you cross.

Walk ahead to another stile. This one is straightforward and has no wire. Continue onto the gated access track and follow it as it swings right until you reach Roman Road, where you turn right. Step out along this quiet lane, where pied wagtails have already started to nest. Ignore the first right turn and take the cart-track on the right, signposted Light Trees.

Stride the track until you come close to the Dowgill Beck just before the farm. Look upstream to see the greatest reward of this walk. The beck descends through its steep tree-lined gill in a series of foaming falls. Sit on a convenient boulder and enjoy this turbulent stream, which rages, boils, cascades, plummets and swirls in great haste to add its waters to the Argill, deep in the nature reserve visited earlier.

Cross the beck by the tractor bridge and bear left to pick up the track that climbs the slope to the gate taken earlier. Turn left to walk the track to regain your car.

Low Force

4. Low Force and Summerhill Force, Upper Teesdale

GRs 902281, 909287, 10 miles

PARK IN front of Hill Terrace, Middleton in Teesdale. Leave the centre of the town by the B6277 (south-west corner of the Terrace) and cross Middleton Bridge over the surging River Tees. Beyond, turn right along the Pennine Way. The path is easy to follow, and in early spring the grass grows vigorously. The path crosses pastures where each boundary wall has its own stile.

Continue along the path, where ash and wych elm shade the

way. Sometimes steep tree-clad slopes drop down to the stately river and through the bare branches a pair of dippers can be seen flitting from boulder to boulder, flying downstream.

Follow the way as it leaves the river side for a short distance. Here, high in tall ash trees and about the pastures, hundreds of fieldfare feed. They flit in small restless flocks from tree to field, calling loudly. Perhaps this is their gathering point before their migration to the continent.

The path crosses diagonally to the side of Park End Wood, where long tailed tits pass through the trees. As the path returns close to the winding Tees but high above it oyster catchers pipe from meadows on the opposite bank. Away to the right curlews call from the open fell and here too a very young lamb snuggles close to its Swaledale mother.

The path drops down through trees to a footbridge over Eel Beck and two ladder stiles lead to the side of the river, which is very wide. Look for the pair of grey wagtails flitting from one large cobble to the next. Continue past Newbiggin Bridge, where the pink flowers of the larch have appeared on twigs now covered with delicate needles.

Walk on past falls where the Tees foams white and the water is streaked with peat stain and where huge Scots pine, on the opposite bank provide a magnificent backdrop. Coltsfoot,

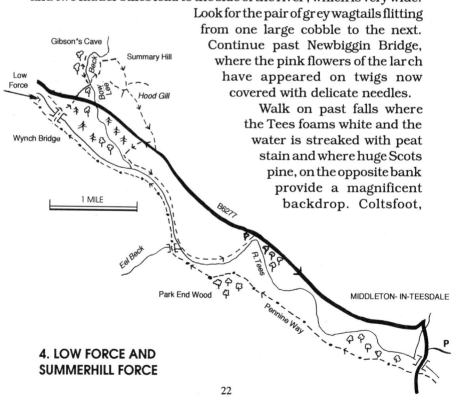

**4. LOW FORCE AND
SUMMERHILL FORCE**

Long tailed tits . . . oyster catchers

wood anemones and kingcups flower beside the path as it passes more rapids. Look for bilberry, heavy with tiny pink flowers, growing about a craggy overhang.

Cross the chain suspension Wynch Bridge and walk upstream past cascades and rapids to Low Force. The beck descends in a series of foaming falls, coffee streaked. Sit on a rocky ledge and watch the lovely river race between confining walls composed of six-sided boulders. Look for the dippers feeding in the shallows and for the pair of tree creepers ascending the rough bark of the trees close by.

The path passes through the trees to a gap stile in a wall. Cross the pasture beyond, where green plovers court, to a signposted gate to the road. Cross to the other side and walk uphill to the Bowlees Visitor Centre housed in an old methodist church. Take the path to the right of the centre to the car park and turn left to follow the nature trail. Walk past a charming double cascade beneath willow, beech, wych elm and pine where the song of a wren fills the air.

Continue upstream another 100yds to Summerhill Fall, where Bow Lee Beck drops in two elegant falls over a huge amphitheatre of layered rock. Beneath, where the stream has worn away the rock, is Gibson's cave, once the hiding place of a sixteenth-century outlaw. The fall lies in a lovely tree filled hollow, with primroses in full flower. This is a place to linger.

Return to the car park and turn left and take a signposted path to Summary Hill. Don't miss the grassy path off to the right, to a way-marked gate, where the cart track makes a large turn to

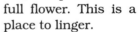

23

the left. Pass behind the cottages at Hood Gill, where another pair of grey wagtails prospect for a nesting site. Continue to a gate onto the lane leading down into Newbiggin. Take the second turn on the right to pass an interesting old methodist chapel. At the lane end turn right and walk back 100yds along the B6277 to the footpath on the opposite side of the road.

Walk across the pasture and pass through a gap stile to a shady walled track. Turn left over a stile just before the footbridge and continue beside the Bow Lee river once more. The way is gated and stiled and continues beside the River Tees once the confluence of the two becks is passed. More and more stiles have to be climbed but the path beside the wide gracious river is a joy to walk. Redshanks and oyster catchers feed in nearby pastures and many ewes are busy with tiny lambs.

The path leads into a small wood carpeted with butterbur. Follow the waymarks through the trees. The exit to the road lies at the far left hand corner of the wood. Turn right. From here it is 1½ miles to Middleton-in-Teesdale.

Gibson's cave and Summerhill Force

Falls below bridge on Hudeshope Beck

5. Horseshoe Falls on Hudeshope Beck, Upper Teesdale

GR 948268, 6 miles

THIS WALK takes you through glorious woodland, over quiet pastures, out onto a wild moorland road, past lead mining country and through a hidden valley where the Hudeshope Beck tumbles in many delightful falls.

Park in front of Hill Terrace in the centre of Middleton-in-Teesdale, where raucous rooks attend to their rookeries in the huge trees. Turn left to pass the ornate Bainbridge drinking fountain, erected in 1875. Follow the B6277, along Market Place, and continue across the bridge over the Hudeshope Beck. Just beyond, begin the steep climb up The Hude, signposted Middleside - this continues straight ahead where the B6277 swings sharply left. Opposite Chapel Cottage take the stone steps which climb uphill between the houses on the right side of The Hude, from where you have a good view of the rooftops of the town.

Walk along the continuing path to join a forest track through the deciduous woodland. Look down the steep slope on the right to the Hudeshope, where it descends in a white-topped fall. Where the track divides, take the left branch that

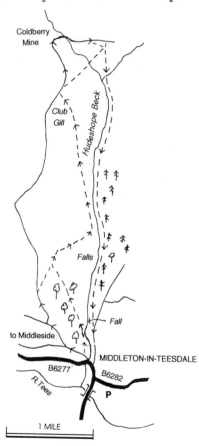

5. HORSESHOE FALLS

continues by the boundary wall. Celandines, dog's mercury and the ubiquitous ransomes cover the forest floor.

Pass through the gate into a pasture, which is full of ewes and lambs, and walk ahead towards a derelict building in the right-hand corner. Pass through the stile behind the building and walk ahead, bearing slightly to the left, to a stile to the right of a gate. Follow the wall on the right and take the stile half-way along the wall. Beyond, continue beside the wall, now on your left, and walk to the gate to the left of Aukside Villa, with a huge monkey puzzle tree in its front garden. (The footpath from the gate out of the forest and across the pastures to Aukside is waymarked, but, unfortunately, on the far side of the stiles and gates!)

Walk ahead to pass through a gate, turn right and stroll through the hamlet of Aukside. Where the lane turns left, look on the right side for the stone-stepped stile, to the left of some outhouses. Cross the pasture beyond, diagonally right, to a stile in the corner and do the same in the next pasture. This gives access to the steep-sided How Gill, down which races a narrow stream. Head right down the steep slope and step across the hurrying water, just above its union with the Hudeshope Beck, and continue upstream.

Enjoy this glorious hollow, where the Hudeshope descends in foaming cascades below an attractive stone bridge. Walk along the path and pass through the gate on the right onto a quarry road. Look across to the slopes on the right to see six magnificent lime kilns set into the hillside.

Turn left at the gate and walk on along the reinforced track, which is lined with young firs and larches on the left and deciduous trees on the right. Here willow warblers proclaim their arrival with their liquid song. The track moves into a hollow with larch and Scots pine on both sides.

Walk on to cross a tiny stream and climb a waymarked stile on the left. Ascend the slope ahead. Just beyond the next waymarked stile climb right, passing through young larch and treading on wild strawberry flowers spreading across the path, to a stile over the fence ahead and another over the wall beyond.

Stride ahead from the two stiles to pass through three stiles in the boundary walls ahead. Walk diagonally left towards a gap stile silhouetted on the skyline. In this extensive pasture a bull grazes peacefully surrounded by his cows and calves. The pasture is slashed by the steep-sided Clubgill, through which flows a narrow stream. Beyond the newly restored gap stile, seen earlier, walk diagonally left to the signposted gap stile to the road, passing the white painted Club Gill farmhouse on the left.

Turn right along the narrow road as it curves round the head of the valley. It passes the Coldberry Lead Mine, one of the largest in Teesdale, which closed in 1955. Here you can see semi-derelict buildings, regular-shaped spoil heaps, dressing floors and pieces of machinery scattered over the scarred hill slopes overlooking the Hudeshope Beck. What a noise and a bustle there must have been not so many years ago. Now only the bubbling calls of curlews and the haunting songs of redshanks break the silence of this lonely moorland.

After crossing over the Hudeshope Beck stride on past the track to Pikestone Brow Farm. Just beyond, opposite a planting of new trees still hidden by their biodegradable sleeves, strike off right across the rough pasture. Cross an unnamed stream and continue to a waymarked stile in the wall ahead. Beyond drop down to cross the Marl Beck - which, if in spate, might require wading!

Continue along the wide grassy track to a gap in the wall and then through the next waymarked gap. Continue to a stone building to see a beautifully constructed adit or tunnel into the mine, from which comes a continuous flow of icy water. Walk on to see another adit to the right. High in the larches ahead two male ring ousels fight for a territory. They crash through the branches, scolding harshly, and then fly to nearby larches to continue their aggression. Eventually one flies off down the valley, leaving the victor to advertise for a mate with its loud, clear song (see p6).

Follow the track up to a wooden gate. Walk on and leave the track by a waymarked path on the right. Continue ahead along the waymarked stiled path, within sound of the Hudeshope Beck, to a waymarked ladder stile into Snaisgill Plantation. Walk the level path through the glorious woodland, high above the beck. Then drop down steeply to the grassy floor of the disused Skears Quarry, where primroses grow. Follow the path out of the quarry to come to the top of the limekilns, seen earlier. Look for the holes at the top through which lumps of limestone and fuel were dropped.

Continue along the quarry road or along the narrow path beside the hurrying river. Here flower huge clumps of white violets. Walk on to a point just beyond a bench seat at the side of the r oad. Here a path leads down to the bed of the river and a good view of the delightful Horseshoe Falls. The Hudeshope surges over plates of limestone, in a mass of white foam and spray. Along the riverbank, it continually erodes the softer rock below the limestone, forming caves, until the plates collapse onto the river bed. Pause her e to enjoy these grand falls. Look at the boulders along the bed to find interesting fossils. Notice the dipper that hurriedly flies upstr eam.

Follow the quarry road to Stanhope Road. Turn right and walk downhill to Market Place.

ring ouzel . . .
"its loud, clear song"(walk 5)

White Force
32

6. White Force, Upper Teesdale

GR 852280, 7 miles

T HE FIRST part of this walk takes you beside the stately River Tees. The second part, to see White Force, leads you over the airy moorland of Cronkley Fell, using an old drove road.

Park at the small Hanging Shaw picnic area, Forest in Teesdale, 2 miles west of High Force, on the B6277. From here there is a grand view of Holwick Fell, Noon Hill, White Force, Cronkley Fell, Holmwath and Widdybank Fell. Cross the road and walk right to a signpost. Turn left and walk the farm track towards Birk Rigg. Here in the pastures a dozen plovers dive acrobatically and give their wild musical whistle.

Walk to the left of the farmhouse. Cross a small stone arched bridge, one of several where tracks cross and recross a narrow stream. Pass through the gate beyond and the one almost immediately to the right. Turn left and walk towards Wat Garth farm. Follow the path as it swings right to cross another arched bridge. Pass through two gates and turn left. Walk down the slope to a row of large sandstone stepping stones taking you across a marshy area spangled with kingcups.

Cross Cronkley Bridge, which spans the wide, noisy, peat-

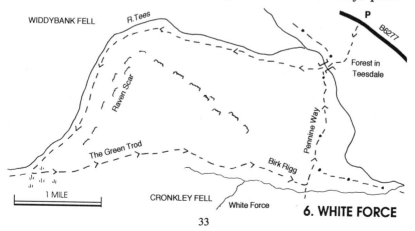

6. WHITE FORCE

stained Tees where its waters swirl angrily against the many boulders in its way. A few yards on, pass right through the unsignposted double metal gates and walk ahead, over closely cropped pasture, keeping a wall to the left. Bear left where the wall turns left, and then right, keeping to the side of a drainage ditch. Continue along a causeway that leads towards a stone barn. Pass through a gate just before the barn, turn right and walk ahead towards the river.

Step out along the path beside the racing water where redshanks feed and black-headed gulls preen on rocks. Continue beside the ruin of the old Pencil Mill. Here outcropped the soft blue slate (rock formed 500 million years ago) which was used for the manufacture of slate pencils. Walk on beside two islands in the river where oyster catchers probe along the shingle reaches and curlews fly overhead. Then a little boulder hopping is required before the path continues.

As you walk on, Widdy Bank Farm comes into view on the opposite bank. From now on expect to be startled by the noisy alarm call and scolding "go-back" of innumerable grouse. Each richly coloured bird rises when disturbed and flies off just above the heather. It alights at a safe distance and is rapidly lost to sight.

Climb the stile over a drystone wall and use the well-placed duckboards, then boulder hop. To the left looms Raven Scar. After 2 miles of walking beside this lovely river the Falcon Clints, composed of the very hard whin sill, are seen on your right.

Look here for a large island, well-covered with juniper trees and a solitary rowan. At this point strike left over the marshy ground towards a large cairn that indicates the point where the old drove road begins its ascent. The road, known as The Green Trod, once resounded to the calls of drovers as they herded their cattle from Alston to Thirsk.

The wide, stony, grass track climbs steadily towards a cairn on the horizon, named Man Gate on the map. Beyond this point the cairned track continues. Pass the first of four enclosures, wired by the Nature Conservancy Council to prevent further erosion of the sugar limestone by rabbits and sheep. Another gentle climb brings you to the highest point of the trod, with dramatic views of the hills around and a first glimpse of Cow Green reservoir and its dam.

Close by the next enclosure look right to an area of coarse grass, crowberry and stunted ling to see several pairs of golden plovers. These call quietly and clearly as they circle. As they alight their white underwings are revealed. Then their golden backs catch the sun and you can see their black breasts.

Step out along the gently descending path, now a very wide grassy swathe, between huge mats of heather. Look right to see White Force, an elegant waterfall that carries the united waters of Back Sike and Black Ark over the lip of Whin Sill. It drops in a great flurry of white foam to fall into a deep fissure in the sugar limestone. After much rain it flows down the latter and tumbles on over a stony bed. Often the water disappears into the fissure and is lost underground, reappearing 200yds further down the valley.

To see this magnificent fall more closely, turn right along a path. Walk past the spoil heap of an old lead mine and continue to the foot of the fall. From here there is a good view of the fault line between the whin sill and the sugar limestone. Look for a pair of ring ousels flitting about the heather and settling on an old derelict wall.

Return to the trod and walk on. At the Nature Reserve board, turn left and walk towards a waymarked gate, astride the Fell Dike Sike (more boulder hopping required here). Walk up the slope ahead to a waymarked post and then head off the slope, left, to a stile in the corner of the pasture. Beyond, turn right and use the duckboards to climb another slope. Drop downhill and use more duckboards to a stile in the wall on the right.

Turn left (duckboards again), and then begin a rough stony descent. At the bottom, pass through a gate on the left with an acorn sign on it. Walk up beside the wall on the right to pass through a gate beside Cronkley Farm. Turn left and walk along the farm track to Cronkley Bridge. Retrace your outward route to the car park.

"black-headed gulls preen on rocks"

Great Eggleshope Beck

7. Black Force on Great Eggleshope Beck, Upper Teesdale

GR 961312, 6 miles

L EAVE MIDDLETON-IN-TEESDALE by the road to Stanhope and park on a wide verge just before Great Eggleshope Bridge. Cross the bridge and take a wide cart track on the left just before the whitewashed Middle End Farm.

A notice at the start of the walled track reminds walkers that this is a sensitive area for all upland birds and is managed for grouse and sheep. It requests that they stay on footpaths and bridlepaths and keep all dogs on leads. Continue along the wide reinforced track, its verges brightened with violets. Sheep and lambs graze the pastures on either side where green plovers and curlews court and call.

Pass through the gate and continue along the track as it comes close to the hurrying Great Eggleshope Beck. Cross the ford, the bed of which is reinforced with stone for vehicles. Crossing might present problems if the beck is in spate as a huge sleeper, used as a bridge, has fallen into the water. Beyond, continue along the track as it passes through the spoil heaps of a disused lead mine and beside mine buildings, now used to store fodder. Step out along the track to ford the beck again. Here there is another wooden sleeper, rotten in parts, which this time enables you to cross dryshod.

Beyond the ford, three tracks meet. Note this point for the return route. Head left along the lowest track past an adit with water gushing forth. Many of these small entrances to mine levels look most inviting, but they are in poor repair and entry should not be attempted. Ford the beck again and continue to a gate. Beyond lies yet another ford over which to wade or boulder hop, depending on your footwear.

Continue along the mine track as it climbs a little above the beck, into the heart of the gently rounded fells. From the slopes come the calls of curlews, meadow pipits, and wheatears.

Walk on past another well-preserved adit with a fern garden

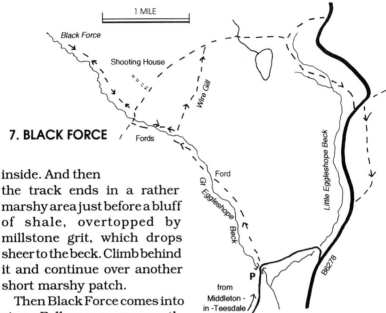

7. BLACK FORCE

inside. And then the track ends in a rather marshy area just before a bluff of shale, overtopped by millstone grit, which drops sheer to the beck. Climb behind it and continue over another short marshy patch.

Then Black Force comes into view. Follow a narrow path, through heather and bilberry, as it climbs again. Str oll on as the path continues along the top of the small gor ge above this small but glorious waterfall.

The Great Eggleshope Beck (which has wetted your boots four times on the walk) winds through the lonely fells and then descends a series of steps in its bed, foaming over each in tur n. It then drops in a wide curtain of peat-stained water to fall into a deep pool. Rowans, in tiny leaf, lean over the for ce and more trees line the banks as the moorland str eam tumbles on. The sides of the tiny gorge are lined with liverworts, thriving in the continual spray. A wren sings loudly from a solitary silver bir ch. What a contrast, after so much industrial der eliction (interesting as it is), to see nature's perfection.

Return to the junction of tracks passed earlier and take the one that continues north into mor e mine workings (ignoring the reinforced track to the Shooting House). Follow the wide track to a gate. Beyond, take the raised, buttr essed path that climbs steadily through Wire Gill. Wood sorrel flowers along its edge. Two male ring ousels flit angrily about it, disputing territorial

38

boundaries. Meadow pipits ascend trilling into the air and then descend with wings outspread. Wheatears fly from boulder to boulder, wary of intruders.

Look for a pretty fall to the left and a well-constructed adit to the right. Just beyond the track swings to the right and comes to the side of a tiny stream. Cross, with a step, and continue ahead. Very quickly the managed path stretches ahead through the heather. Walk along this lovely airy upland way, with extensive heather moorland all around. Overhead a peregrine beats the air with its wings and then holds them steady in a bow before it dives headlong after prey.

Step across another narrow dike and stride out ahead. This leads you close to a small reservoir where black headed gulls circle above the grey water and a pair of tufted ducks stay close. Follow the path as it drops downhill to a fence-stile. Beyond, turn right to walk a wide track through more disused mine workings beside the Little Eggleshope Beck.

Follow the track until you reach the B6278. Turn left and walk back a few yards. Cross the road, with care, on the bend and take a wide grassy track on the right that runs parallel with the road. Stride along this as it begins to descend through the heather. After ¹/₂ mile this track rejoins the road. Continue downhill and take the right turn, signposted Middleton-in-Teesdale. Cross the bridge over the beck, with a pretty fall beneath. Walk on past Middle End Farm to return to your car.

Mine adit

Sedling Burn, Cowshill, Weardale

40

8. Killhope Burn, Cowshill, Weardale

GR 855406, 3 miles

PARK IN the car park at Cowshill on the A689, 11 miles south-east of Alston. Turn right out of the car park and look upstream over the bridge to see an elegant fall on the Sedling Burn. It tumbles white-topped and foaming as it descends through a narrow ravine hidden deep in luxuriant spring vegetation. Cross the road and take the lower road that passes in front of the St Thomas's Church and continues through the brownstone village, where hawthorn and horsechestnut are in flower and rooks call from a nearby rookery.

Turn left into a lane, signposted Burtreeford, and walk to cross the bridge over the Killhope Burn. Pastures stretch into the distance overlooked by steep fells. Turn left beyond the bridge into a gate to join the Weardale Way. Walk forward to pass through the next gate under a sycamore. Look down into the gorge on your left, where the Killhope descends in a dramatic fall. It plummets in one continuous unbroken jet over limestone blocks, dark with water and encrusted with algae. It crashes onto a ledge and then continues in lacy cascades into a deep pool.

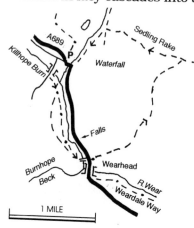

8. KILLHOPE BURN

The rocks forming an amphitheatre have been undercut by the burn, which is spectacular in May, when the volume of water is slight, and which must be even more spectacular when in spate. Cottages stand high above the fall and a cherry tree sheds its petals on the water.

Turn right and walk the high-level path above the burn and then bear left, downhill, to a white painted kissing-gate. Listen for the mellow songs of

41

Cherry blossom

garden warblers in the bushes about the burn. Continue, to climb a stile in the wall ahead. By the next stile look for the pretty horseshoe-shaped falls. Beyond, continue to a signposted gate and turn left to cross the bridge into the village of Wearhead. Here the Burnhope Burn joins the Killhope and forms the River Wear.

Turn right into Front Street and walk through the tiny village to take a signposted left turn opposite the phone box. Climb the cart-track and continue ahead over a stile. Walk on up the slopes, where huge mats of the lovely mountain pansy grow, some yellow, others purple and white, yet more almost pink. Continue beyond the next gate. Walk up the slope, where a pair of partridge fly off with creaking voice and whirring wings. Continue to a signposted stile to the road, keeping to the left of a house. Walk right and then, in 10yds, turn left into a gated track.

Walk up the track, and follow it where it swings to the right past Halliwell House. Here a blackcock flies low over the wall. Pass through the next gate onto moorland, about which fly meadow pipits, green plovers, skylarks and curlews. Follow the cart-track, keeping beside the wall on the right. Look back for a good view of the Burnhope Reservoir, a triangle of blue edged with conifers and set in a hollow in the hills. Pass through the next gate and walk on, now with the wall on your left. Pass through another gate to join Sedling Rake - a wide, walled grassy track from where there are wonderful views of upper Weardale.

Turn left through another gate to walk the rake (Wear Valley Way) as it begins its rough descent towards Cowshill. Look for the litter of purple-tinged fluorspar strewn along the way. Walk downhill through the spoil tips, from the Sedling Vein where lead was obtained. The tips are now transformed by vast numbers of mountain pansy. Look down right to see Sedling Burn descend in a stream of foaming water beneath sycamores and a Scots pine into a dark hollow of shale.

Continue down the track past the spoil heaps of Burntree Pasture Mine. Follow it as it swings left to come close to the Sedling Burn and walk the mine track to the car park at Cowshill.

First waterfall seen on Flushiemere Beck walk

44

9. Flushiemere Beck, Bowlees, Upper Teesdale

GRs 908293, 910298, 5¹/₂ miles

PARK IN the car park of Bowlees picnic site. Return to the information centre, a former Methodist chapel, and walk past the front of it to a gate. Beyond, bear right to walk up a slope along a wide track. Mixed woodland lies to the right and pastures, criss-crossed with walls and with a scattering of white-washed barns, stretch away to the left. Pass through a gate and continue on. Go through another with a waymark on the far side.

Follow the faint track left and then strike right across the pasture. Drop down the steepish slope to cross Causeway Sike. Climb up the other side, past spotted orchids, wild strawberry and violets, to cross the stile in the wall. Continue ahead, with the wall to the right, to a stile in the wall ahead. Pause on the stile to look ahead to a pretty fall on Flushiemere Beck.

Beyond the stile walk ahead for 50yds and then turn right (east), and walk along the top of a spur that drops downhill to the side of Wester Beck. Step across and climb over the fence where it joins a wall and where the barbed wire has been removed so that you can continue on the right of way.

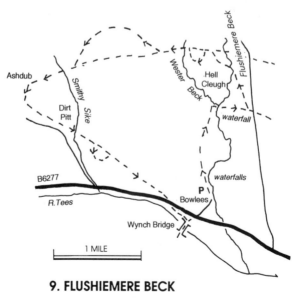

9. FLUSHIEMERE BECK

45

Beyond the fence, turn right and follow the faint path over a small outcrop. Then drop down to a charming fall on Flushiemere Beck. Here the stream hurries in lacy cascades over water-blackened rocks. Birch and willow in delicate new leaf shade the water and the banks are covered with primroses. Cross the beck on rocks just above the waterfall.

This is the point to which to return after you have made a short diversion up the gill. Walk upstream to another pleasing fall below a tall crag which supports rowan, birch and bird cherry. A spotted flycatcher calls for a mate from the topmost branch. Look for fossils in the boulders which line the beck.

Continue through the glorious wooded gill to see the waterfall from the top of the stile. Here a series of small cascades descends over rock ledges. Continue upstream, through wood sorrel, to see another elegant fall that foams and sprays as it hurries down its rocky bed. A dipper flies from the side of the cascades and flies downstream.

Return through the sorrel to the first fall and, continuing in the same easterly direction, climb the slope to a stile beside a large corrugated iron barn. The far side of the stile can be very muddy underfoot - so be warned. Stride on in the same direction to pass through a gap in the wall ahead. Walk on where green plovers wheel and call to distract intruders from their nests. Where the moorland road comes into sight, turn left to climb the sloping pasture, keeping to the right of a stone sheep-pen. Pass through the stile in the far left corner of the wall ahead.

Again pause on the stile for an exciting view of a splendid waterfall on the Flushiemere Beck. The mountain stream hurries through the gill before descending in one long jet of foaming water, each droplet catching the sunlight. The water is channelled between large blocks of limestone into a deep pool which foams and seethes. From here a female ring ousel scolds angrily and then flies down the gill. Rowans and silver birch line the sides of the gorge, which is called Hell Cleugh. With the sun turning each pale leaf translucent, this glorious corner of Teesdale should perhaps be renamed Paradise Cleugh.

Walk on towards the footbridge, past an adit - an entrance to an old lead mine. The stones of the entrance are covered with liverworts, ferns and wood sorrel, luxuriating in the sheltered environment. Cross the waymarked bridge and climb the slope to a stile in the wall. Bear right to a gate in the wall to the right of Broadley's Farm. Walk ahead to the gate opposite, which gives access to a farm-track. Redshanks sit on the wall and gate and fly off uttering their long melodious cries. 20yds along the track, pass through the gate on the left.

The right-of-way on the map leads to the far right cor ner but there is no way to get over the wall. Instead walk r ound the end of a wall that ends in the middle of the pastur e. Then head right to a gate in the wall on the right. Beyond dr op down the slope to step across Wester Beck, which you crossed earlier. Pass through the red metal gate in the wall ahead into a huge pastur e where the air resounds with the calls of curlews, gr een plovers and skylarks.

Continue ahead and pass through another gate, just after you have stepped over a narrow stream or sike. Beyond continue ahead. Here again the right-of-way on the map strikes diagonally left to a wall with no way of cr ossing it. Instead pass through a gate in the far boundary wall and then bear left. Cr oss three more sikes to come to a gate in the wall. T o the right stand several Scots pine and here a black cock feeds on pine needles. It is in the pastur e just crossed that the male bir ds hold their "lek" - a gathering wher e they fight, dance and show off to gain the appr oval of the watching females.

Beyond the gate, drop down the hill, keeping parallel to a wall on the right. Cross over a narr ow sike to a gate in a wir e fence. Walk ahead to pass through a gate in the wall on the right. Continue along the farm track beyond, which leads to Ashdub. Keep to the left of the farmhouse to drop down the access track. Follow this as it swings left to cross a bridge over Etters Beck. Continue ahead along the track, with the delightful tr ee-lined beck dancing along to your left.

Look left to see another adit on the far side of the beck, with spoil heaps on either side. Walk on to the small hamlet of Dirt Pitt, meaning deer path. Turn left to cr oss the bridge over the beck and continue along the r einforced lane. Cross Smithy Sike, climb up the hill and take the gate on the right. Strike left and climb the small slope to pass through a gate (the stile has been blocked).

Beyond, strike left to a stone stepped stile - it is to the right of a gate. Once over, walk ahead, keeping the wall and then the plantation to the left. Pass through the gate and keep to the right of East Friar House. Continue along the gated track to where it swings right, where you walk ahead. Pass through a gate and then continue ahead to drop down through trees to a stile to the road. Cross and turn left to take the signposted footpath which leads to the side of the lovely River Tees.

Walk downstream along the treelined banks, where bluebells fill the air with perfume and cowslips grow, until you reach the magnificent Low Force. Stand on the Wynch Bridge for a wonderful view of this lovely part of the river. Return to the bank and take the path up through the trees to a stile into a pasture. Continue to the road, which you cross. Turn right and almost immediately left to return to the picnic site and your car.

"a spotted flycatcher calls"

Waterfall in the gardens of Eggleston Hall

10. Raygill, near Romaldkirk and falls above Eggleston Bridge

GR 012219, 5 miles

THE PUBLIC car park at Romaldkirk lies behind the Rose and Crown in the centre of this charming village. The latter has three large greens, one with a modern version of stocks and another with a splendid pump. Before you start your walk visit the magnificent twelfth-century St Romald's church, overlooking the lower green. Recently arrived swifts have already established a nest over the porch in front of the Norman doorway. Inside look for the Devil's door - traditionally the devil was supposed to be behind it and it was blocked in late medieval times to keep him out.

Leave the church, walk ahead across the green and take the signposted footpath to the left of Rose Stile cottage. Trees border the path and jack-by-the-hedge, forget-me-nots and greater stitchwort fill the verges. Take the left of two gates at the end of the path and bear diagonally left across the pasture to a gate. Enjoy the peacefulness of this lovely corner of Teesdale.

Continue in the same direction to a waymarked gated gap stile and drop down the slope to the derelict farm of Low Garth. From here you can hear the River Tees noisily descending rapids. Climb the stile just beyond the farm to cross the next pasture, where cowslips, bugle, violets, primroses and bloody cranesbill grow. Pass through the waymarked gate in the far left corner into glorious May woodland. Follow the path through bluebells, rhododendrons, water avens and primroses.

The path comes close to the mighty Tees, where sandpipers flit about the boulders below more rapids. Continue through this glorious flower garden, as the path begins to climb above the now tranquil, stately river. Walk the high level path with care after rain as the slope down to the water is precipitous.

Then the way drops through a great carpet of wild garlic to the edge of more rapids. Look here for curiously eroded rocks, known as fairy cupboards, lining the river bank, and then walk on through sweet cicely and bitter vetch. Above the noise of the river the air is filled with the wonderfully sweet songs of willow warblers and the rich, clear calls of blackcaps. Follow the path through bluebells and pink campion as it climbs to a gate out of the wood.

Walk ahead to a stile and beyond join a farm track. Pass between a row of magnificent beech trees and some farm outbuildings. Continue past a dwelling and along a cobbled yard to walk to a white gate. Follow a wall round to the left, passing in front of a large dwelling to a gate on the left in the wall ahead. Pass through the next gate to enter pleasing parkland pasture where large mats of bluebells grow below oaks in pale green leaf.

Climb the stile in the far left corner, cross Wilden Beck on stepping stones and walk up the sandstone steps ahead. Follow the path, now close beside the Tees, where the deep, dark surging river reflects the glory of kingcups. Cross a stile on the right and continue through a pasture, in the same direction, to a waymarked stile into more deciduous woodland. The path through the wild garlic leads to a footbridge over the Tees - here very wide.

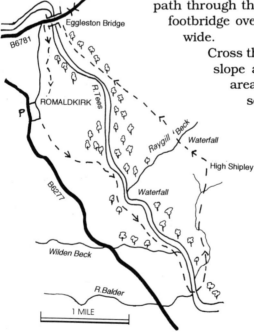

Cross the bridge and climb the slope ahead through a large area of gorse covered with scented golden blossoms. Follow the path as it veers, still climbing, to the left. It joins a cart track and leads to a stile into a caravan site. Walk straight ahead to take a track, through more gorse, that climbs a slope to a waymarked gate.

Beyond, climb the pasture. Pause here to look left to see the flat tops of Goldsborough and Shacklesborough.

10. RAYGILL

Below lies the brown stone village of Cotherstone. Pass through the stone stile in the top left corner, which leads into deciduous woodland. Turn right to follow the path beside the boundary wall. Look left to see a pretty waterfall, on a stream that you will cross and recross later, and then climb a stile out of the wood.

Turn left and, keeping to the left of a hedge and the stream, follow the path until you reach a wall. Continue beside the wall, which is now on your left, to a signposted gate in a wall ahead. Strike diagonally right towards the far right corner of the wall ahead, crossing the narrow stream on a stone slab. Just before the signposted gate ahead look for an ancient bloomery littered with slag and cinders from smelting ore. The existence of the bloomery would account for the excellent man-made raised path, sited well above the small stream.

Pass through the waymarked gate and continue following the waymarks to cross the second of two stone slab bridges over the stream. Then recross it once more by a sturdy wooden footbridge. Here in a wet area grow cuckoo-flowers, which attract a host of orange tip butterflies.

Beyond the footbridge, cross the stile ahead and follow the signpost directions, diagonally left up the slope to a gate in the top left corner. Walk left onto a narrow lane and look left to High Shipley with a plaque in the wall, dated 1670. The farm is thought to have been built for Richard III, and was given to Miles Forest for his alleged part in the murder of the Princess in the Tower. The theory goes that High Shipley was far enough from London to keep the murderer out of the way, and attractive enough to keep him silent.

Turn left into the pathway to walk between the farmhouse and its outbuildings to a waymarked gate beyond. Pass through another farm gate and then step out across a pasture spangled with dandelions to a white gate half way along the wall ahead.

Strike diagonally left to a signposted stile. Beyond lies the waterfall, the focal point of the walk. The Raygill Beck unassumingly crosses the pasture before it drops in great exuberance down a sheer-sided narrow ravine. The long thin stream of white spray splashes over water-blackened rock where pink campion, forget-me-nots, greater stitchwort and cuckoo-flower thrive in the tiny droplets that fill this pretty hollow. Elms line the slopes but alas several have died and their timber litters the gill bottom.

Cross the little beck and strike across the pastures, where curlews call. The gate lies half way along the boundary wall ahead. Walk ahead to pass in front of East Barnley farmhouse. Beyond, bear diagonally left to a waymarked gate. Continue in the same direction to a stile beneath more dead elms and walk on, now within sound of the River Tees once more. Continue to a gate into bluebell woodland. Drop down the steps to cross above another waterfall, and then follow the stepped path downhill to a tarmacked road. Turn right and walk to Eggleston Bridge.

Here make a short diversion to the right. Walk uphill towards the two arched bridge. Look over the wall to see a splendid fall, tumbling in great haste below the bridge. Continue uphill to a magnificent waterfall on the right, in the grounds of Eggleston Hall. Here a spotted flycatcher sits on a dead branch and gives the few soft notes of its oft repeated call.

Return down the hill to cross the narrow bridge, originally built in the fifteenth century, over the Tees. Climb the road to take a signposted footpath on the left. Walk ahead and follow the path beside the wall on the left. Cross the waymarked stile and then strike diagonally right to the next stile. Beyond, walk ahead. Just after you have passed the burial ground on the right and before you reach Beer Beck, look for a stone stile in the wall to a copse on the left. Turn right to cross the stone bridge over the beck and continue along Primrose Lane to Romaldkirk.

Pump at Romaldkirk

Maizebeck Force

11. Maizebeck Force, Upper Teesdale

GR 802274, 6 miles

START YOUR walk at the Wheelhead Sike car park at Cow Green Reservoir. Follow the signposted directions for Cauldron Snout, Widdybank Fell nature trail and the dam. Look for the abundant mountain pansy, with its deep purple petals, and the small Teesdale violet growing beside the way to the dam. Look, too, to see overhangs of peat and vast clumps of heather spangled with tormentil, and outcrops of sugar-limestone on which thrive many of Teesdale's rare plants.

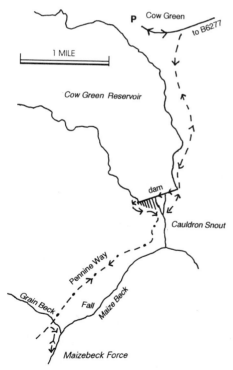

Follow the track as it drops downhill. Once at the dam you may choose to cross it and enjoy grand views of the vast, lonely stretch of water surrounded by remote fells. Or you may prefer to follow the track as it drops down to a bridge over the top of Cauldron Snout (the focal point of walk no: 1). Beyond the bridge the two routes join.

Continue along the cart track, part of the Pennine Way, with the meandering Maize Beck below to the left. Stride along the Way, following the footpath signs. Redshanks flit about the pastures revealing their bright red legs as they drop down to their nests. Curlews fly overhead calling and bubbling as they too return to their young.

11. MAIZEBECK FORCE

Pass in front of Birkdale Farm, where in idyllic June swallows fly in and out of the outbuildings to tend their broods. It is difficult to imagine that in bleak winter the farm is often cut off by snow. Step out across the pasture past golden kingcups and milkmaids. Follow the signpost directions for the Pennine Way to a wooden footbridge over Grain Beck. Cross and turn left to walk beside the hurrying water to its confluence with the Maize.

Walk upstream. Here a pair of grey wagtails flit from rock to rock and sandpipers call from their boulder strewn edge of the river. Pause by a pleasing fall on the Maize and then climb the slope ahead. Beyond lies the magnificent Maizebeck Force. The wide, stately moorland river descends over great plates of rock, cascading in beautiful peat-stained skirts of white water. It is channelled into several chasms before passing into a deep, narrow ravine where it rages furiously, creating a tremendous noise before hurrying to tumble over the shallow falls below.

Return by the same route.

Curlew

Little stream falling into disused quarry

12. Falls near Frosterley, Weardale

GRs 034372, 033361, 3¹/₂ miles

F ROSTERLEY, WEARDALE, is a linear village of sturdy stone dwellings. It is surrounded by many disused quarries from which "marble" and limestone were obtained. Some of the marble was used in Durham Cathedral. Nature has nearly reclaimed most of the quarries.

Park in the public car park in the centre of Frosterley, almost opposite the post office and beside the telephone box and the village hall. Turn left and walk along Front Street and left again to follow the footpath sign, opposite the newspaper shop. Follow the way as it winds left between houses and pass through a gate which gives access to a steep pasture. At the top of the slope sit on the seat and enjoy the grand view of the village and the sloping hills of Weardale beyond. Continue to the right corner to a waymarked stile at the corner of an old quarry, now colonised by tall trees and summer vegetation. Carry on along the narrow path, which is lined with bluebells, cowslips, cow parsely, wood avens, greater stitchwort and woody cranesbill, to another waymarked stile.

Bear left and just beyond two large ash trees strike right up the slope to join a track. Follow it right and pass through a gate to walk on with a wall to your right. Where the track swings left, head on, still keeping to the side of the wall. Here, on this high level way, with magnificent views of Weardale, you are among green plovers and curlews busy with their broods. Pass through another gate and follow the track to a stile beside the next gate. Carry on towards a ruined barn and, just before, stride the track as it curves right to a gate.

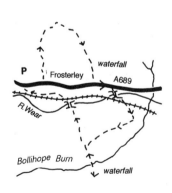

12. FALLS NEAR FROSTERLEY

Woody cranesbill

Beyond, bear left to a gap close to a row of ash and continue on the same diagonal to a stile to the left of a group of trees. Dawdle on with a small stream to your right to a gate. Beyond, look over the fence to see the hurrying water disappear over the lip of another old quarry, now pleasingly grassed and with its rock faces supporting trees and bushes. Pass on to the busy A689. Here walk back, right, to the centre of a small group of houses and between these you can see the charming 100ft drop made by the little stream as it tumbles, with much grace, to the floor of the quarry.

Cross the busy road and walk left and then turn right to stride the bridge over the wide, fast flowing River Wear. Beyond the railway line bear left and walk below an avenue of limes and then out into the open countryside. Pass Broadway House and continue ahead to a waymarked stile. Turn right to walk a track beside another disused quarry, this one not yet taken back by nature. Continue until just before a huge grassed heap of quarry waste on your left, where you turn left. It is easy to miss the waymarking here.

Climb a difficult waymarked stile and pass through the one opposite to cross the footbridge over the Bollihope Burn. Turn right and walk the grassy hollow to the edge of a small feeder stream which hurries in tiny white-topped falls over a series of ledges to lose its energy into the larger burn. Return across the bridge and walk below the bank of waste to rejoin the track. Climb the stile in the corner of the fence.

Keep beside the fence on your right to join a track through yet another disused quarry. All about you lies the quarry debris but gradually tracks, waste heaps and bits of machinery are disappearing beneath the burgeoning plant life. Walk on to pass a two-armed footpath sign and continue to another where you bear to the left for a few yards.

Look for a very narrow path continuing ahead through dense vegetation and beside a fence to your left. Walk to a stile. Pause and enjoy the charming view below. Drop down the steep slope to the side of the River Wear.

Cross the splendid wooden footbridge over the Wear, where wagtails and sandpipers tend their young. Pass through the gate, cross the railway line and follow the track left. Follow the waymarks to pass through a white kissing gate. Carry on over a meadow to another kissing gate. Walk the track behind the church and continue on in front of a row of cottages, with a steep drop left to their gardens. Beyond, where the footpath branches, take a narrow right fork to return to Front Street. Turn right and the car park lies 50yds further on your left.

The waterfall near Stanhope

13: Falls near Stanhope, Weardale

GR 986410 (PF NY 84/94, 570 Allenheads & Rookhope), 4 miles

STANHOPE LIES nearly half way along Weardale. The small town has had a weekly market since the fifteenth century. Its prosperity was once based on lead and iron mining and the quarrying of stone. It has a fine church and a fossil tree thought to be 250 million years old. Today the centre of Stanhope is a conservation area.

Park in the Castle Gardens car park by the Durham Dales centre and turn right to walk 600yds along the A689, passing the Grey Bull pub. Turn right into the signposted way just before Stanhope Old Hall, a massive ancient fortified manor house, now a hotel and restaurant. Walk out into the countryside, with Stanhope Burn to the right. Follow the good track as it keeps beside the hurrying water through the trees of Stanhope Dene, beneath which grows a colourful carpet of summer flowers.

Ignore the right branch to the footbridge and walk on through the lush vegetation. Goldfinches fly up from a buttercup meadow as you follow the path, which is hedged on the right and fenced on the left. Stroll on along the now high-level way under beech and sycamore, where steep wooded slopes drop down to the burn.

Then the track drops to cross two small footbridges where grow bluebells, pink campion, wild garlic, water avens, wood avens and bugle. Continue past a huge fallen tree. Do not cross the next footbridge over the Stanhope but continue along the narrow path with the burn still to the right, following the path as it moves away from the main river to a narrow plank

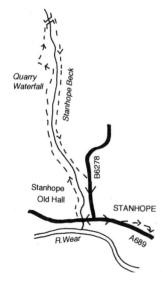

13. STANHOPE

footbridge over a subsidiary stream. Beyond, climb the stepped way until high above the burn once more, where huge beeches grow. Here garden warblers, the nightingales of the north, call.

Follow the path left as it swings away from the burn. Walk with care to the edge of an old quarry to see a charming waterfall, the focal point of the walk. A tributary stream, the haunt of a pair of yellow wagtails, is divided by a bluff of rock into two pretty cascades which descend over steps of limestone. It plummets onto a wider ledge and the water fans out like lace before it meanders through the bottom of the grassy amphitheatre. This lovely fall, set in a glorious hollow, is shadowed by elms, beeches, sycamores, willow, rowan and gorse. The grassy slopes of the old quarry are a mass of primroses, violets and wood sorrel.

Continue to a stile on your left and walk on a few yards to turn right to pass through a huge gate. Beyond, cross the bridge over the tumbling stream and head on past Shield Hurst, where a cuckoo calls continuously. Follow the way, which is bordered with a profusion of primroses, as it drops right to cross a bridge over the Stanhope Burn. Turn right to walk through the derelict fluospar mine and then more disused quarries. Here a black cap and a redstart sing.

Stride the now-reinforced mine road and look for the adits to the left. To the right the burn drops in a series of noisy falls. Continue until you reach the Crawley road (B6278), where you turn right and walk downhill. Turn left by the Grey Bull and then take the Back Lane to pass the methodist chapel. At Stone House turn right to walk down Church Lane and pass through the large gate on the right into St Thomas's churchyard. Look for unusual verses on the tombstones. The church was built in about 1200. Walk into the market place to see the stone cross and then turn right to pass the fossil tree and continue to rejoin your car.

Pink campion and bugle

A fall on Rookhope Burn, Weardale

14. Four falls on Rookhope Burn, Eastgate, Weardale

GRs 953389, 954391, 953394, 949399, 2 miles

PARK AS close as you can to Eastgate, a tiny village on the A689 west of Stanhope. Walk north up a narrow lane, east of the Rookhope Burn, to pass a small chapel, built in 1891, on the left and All Saints Church on the right. Where you reach a narrow right turn for the village hall, once the school, turn left. Walk behind two cottages and then turn right, to take steps on the left, behind the old mill. Follow the paved way round to the right of the mill to a splendid wooden footbridge that spans the Rookhope Burn.

From here you have a grand view of the Low Linn Falls, a hidden horseshoe cascade, where the burn hurries over extensive limestone blocks and falls in foaming cascades into a large basin of brown water. Trout leap the falls, many dropping back only to try again. Sycamore, ash, hazel and hawthorn lean over the falls and the hollow seems filled with dappled sunshine and a great noise.

Cross the bridge and turn right to walk the narrow path through the trees to see the delightful High Linn Falls, which have been extensively restored. Here in another quiet tree-girt hollow a family of grey wagtails flit from branch to branch. As a fledgling alights pleading to be fed it elevates and spreads its tail. The canary-yellow of the male catches the sunlight and brightens the shady corner.

Follow the path through the caravan site and cross the stile at the end. Continue on to see another dramatic fall where the Rookhope races over shallow limestone blocks which divide the waters into six small foaming falls. Here a dipper runs into the water, above the fall, to find prey for its brood.

Continue along the path, where meadow saxifrage, violet and bugle grow. Climb a broken stile and walk on into deciduous woodland where primroses and bluebells flower and the river is alder-lined. Continue to the fence ahead. Here the river descends the Turn Wheel waterfall in a flurry of raging water.

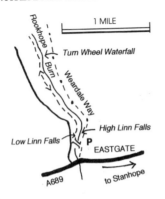

All four falls on the pretty Rookhope are dramatic even after a long dry spell. After rain they are magnificent.

The path continues but after ¹/₂ mile it has been washed away in previous floods. To return, retrace your outward route.

14. ROOKHOPE BURN

Falls on Middlehope Burn

71

15. Middlehope Burn, Westgate, Weardale

GR 905382 (PF NY 84/94, 570 Allenheads & Rookhope, not essential) 3¹/₂ miles

T O REACH the car park on the old station yard at Westgate, turn south by the Hare and Hounds pub. Cross the River Wear, which is very wide and surges strongly here, and turn left into the large gravelled area used for parking. It is not signposted, but appears on the OS map. Westgate is a quiet pleasing linear village situated high in Weardale. It is a popular centre for walking and was once a cock-fighting centre.

Return to the main street and walk left in front of the pub, cross the road and take the first turning on the right, just before the post office. At the bottom of the hill that climbs out into the high pastures above the village, bear left to pass between cottages and an abattoir where the signpost for the Weardale Way is obscured. Pass through the gate into Slit Wood to see the first of many splendid falls on the tempestuous Middlehope Burn.

Dawdle through the glorious woodland to pass a dramatic fall where the raging burn tumbles down limestone steps in a wide peat-stained cascade into a boiling pool, only to plummet yet again over another huge step in its bed. Then, in a series of small cascades, it continues downstream. Stroll on to pass another magnificent horseshoe-shaped waterfall, the water dancing over ledge after ledge.

15. MIDDLEHOPE BURN

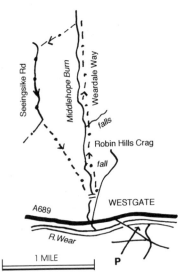

72

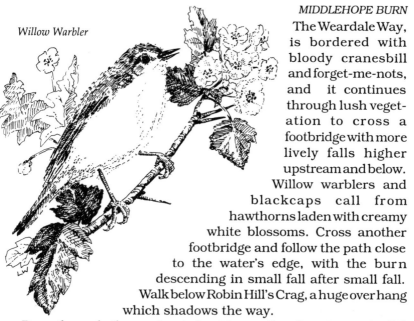

Willow Warbler

MIDDLEHOPE BURN

The Weardale Way, is bordered with bloody cranesbill and forget-me-nots, and it continues through lush vegetation to cross a footbridge with more lively falls higher upstream and below. Willow warblers and blackcaps call from hawthorns laden with creamy white blossoms. Cross another footbridge and follow the path close to the water's edge, with the burn descending in small fall after small fall. Walk below Robin Hill's Crag, a huge overhang which shadows the way.

Pass through the next gate beside another foaming waterfall and walk past loading bays of an old mine. The burn is crossed here on a long turfed foot-bridge. Look for the lovely fall below. Stride on and follow the path, still keeping to the right of the beck.

Straddle the next stile, which leads into more open countryside, with the moors stretching away to the left and ahead. As the path climbs higher above the burn look for another fall where the river races over a semi-circle of rock. Pass more debris of mining and stroll on into moorland. Walk a low causeway between the burn and a water-filled level, where swallows and housemartins fly low over the water and a tree pipit rises into the air and then descends to the tree below with wings extended. Continue through the next waymarked gate.

The way passes a gated adit and then, when you see a water rack across the hurrying stream, drop down to the side of the water to a row of boulders by which you cross the Middlehope. If they are under water then it's off with your boots. Take the path leading left up the slope to a waymarked gate. Walk the wide walled track as it climbs over Middlehope Moor.

At the T-junction, turn left and continue along another wide walled track (Seeingsike Road) across moorland, where curlews call and a hare bounds over the rough pasture. Look right over the wall to see an enormous carpet of mountain pansies.

Where the track begins to descend it becomes edged with trees and bushes. Here a redstart nests. At the two-armed signpost leave the track, which swings right and becomes metalled, to continue ahead to pass through a gate. Walk the reinforced track, which is walled on the left, and follow it as it drops downhill to pass a barn. Just beyond look for the clump of globe flowers growing on the left among the lush vegetation.

Pass through another gate and past a farm to cross a buttercup meadow where hay rattle grows in profusion together with pink clover and eyebright. Beyond the next gate pass below a group of sycamores and descend the slope, where the village comes into view. Pass through the next gate to a farm. Walk ahead, turn left and continue into Westgate. Turn right by the Hare and Hounds to return to the car park.

Fall on Langdon Beck

16. Langdon Beck, Upper Teesdale

GR 855314, 3 miles

PARK BESIDE the Langdon Beck Hotel. Cross the B6277 and walk along the narrow lane that passes between the farm buildings of Wrentnall Farm. Listen here for the noise of the glorious fall on the Langdon Beck. Lean over the wall to see the charming beck descend in a foaming torrent through chasms between great walls of rock where the Langdon negotiates a steep drop in its bed.

A few more steps along the lane look left to see bird's-eye primrose growing along the edge of a small stream - Drygill Sike. On the grassy slopes beyond are deep purple mountain pansies and the pretty pink lousewort flower. Walk on beside Langdon Beck, which is lined with willow, rowan, sycamore and larch and edged with kingcups, blue cranesbill, water avens and gypsywort.

Pass through the various buildings of Valence Lodge and turn right through a metal gate to a bridge over the tree-lined Langdon. Pause here and enjoy the glorious tranquillity. A spotted flycatcher darts after insects with which to feed its fledglings, seemingly precariously balanced on a thin wire stretched across the beck. Two white-washed cottages, one with a rustic porch, nestle in the quiet hollow. Look upstream to a weir with a splendid fall below.

Follow the cart track beyond the bridge, where a pair of mistle thrushes probe the turf for insects. Look left towards the limestone outcrops of High Hurth Edge, with limekilns below. Walk left to a gate onto the slopes below the edge. Beyond, turn right and follow the wall on the right to an ancient gate in a wire fence. Strike uphill, diagonally left, to a gate in the boundary wall ahead. Walk across the pastures,

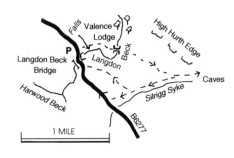

16. LANGDON BECK

where both yellow and purple mountain pansy flower, treading with care. The wet flushes delight the probing snipe. Here it fashions its straw-cup nest in a clump of rough grass. It lays its oval eggs, with the narrow ends pointing to the middle. Continue towards the caves in the limestone cliffs. Peer into the dark recesses and depths but, without the right equipment, do not enter. One of the caves is said to exit in Weardale. Enjoy a good view of the River Tees and Widdy Bank Farm, and also of Cronkley Fell and its slender White Force visited on walk no.6.

To return, drop down the pasture to a gate in the lower boundary wall. Pass through to walk over a magnificent haymeadow where flourish globeflower, hay rattle, meadow saxifrage, kingcups, red clover, buttercups, eyebright and many seeded grasses. Pass through a gate into the next flower bedecked meadow, following the track first to the right beside the wall and then downhill to a gate into Kirkhouse Fold. Follow the rough track, downhill, in front of the old farmhouse, keeping to the right of a wall.

Continue down the farm track, with haymeadows on either side, past the access track to West Underhurth farm. Walk on, now with Silrigg Sike to the left, to pass through a gate. Here a choice awaits you, either to continue the short distance to the road, where you turn right to return to your car, or to turn right and walk the farm track to a dwelling on the right. Beyond a gate, take another track

on the right and walk left, keeping to the right of a wall. Look for the poor step stile towards the end. Then take an even more awkward stile over the next wall on your right - maintaining a direction that is parallel with the road below.

From then on it is easy walking, keeping to the right of the wall to a gate onto Langdon Beck Bridge. From here look upstream for a grand view of the lovely waterfall seen at the start of the walk. Look, too, on either side of the bridge for more spectacular falls where the Langdon continues to descend steeply towards its union with the Harwood Beck.

Gentians

77

Waterfall on How Beck

17. Yawd Sike, West Briscoe, Baldersdale

GR 972186, 7 miles

P ARK IN the car park at the south end of Hury Reservoir
(built in 1894), 4 miles from Cotherstone. Turn left to take
the gated trackway over the top of the dam, where swallows
and wagtails fly overhead. Look across to Shacklesborough and
Goldsborough and to tranquil Baldersdale with its drystone walls
and field barns softened by trees and hedges. Turn left to take the
gated footpath at the end of the dam. (To the right lies a small car
park and a new toilet block.)

Head on, keeping the waters of Hury Reservoir to the left and the
magnificent, if rather ugly, waterboard wall to the right. The way
is grassy and pleasing to walk. It leads a little way into How Gill,
where a wide footbridge takes you across the small stream and
then continues on.

Follow the footpath along the side of a wide inlet to cross a
footbridge, where foxgloves grow in great profusion, just above a
foaming weir. Stride out along
the path until you reach a
wire fence. Walk left

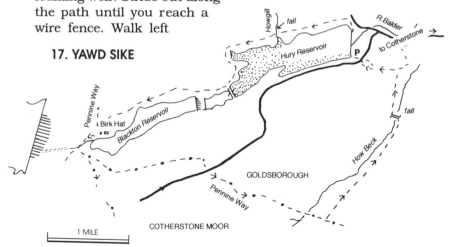

17. YAWD SIKE

1 MILE

79

along a small dam immediately below the much larger dam that holds back the waters of Blackton reservoir. Pass through the gate and turn right to return, over mats of wild thyme, along the dam once more.

Turn left at the end and step out along a track bordered with birch and dog rose heavy with pink blossoms, keeping the small, nameless reservoir to the left and the splendid wall to the right. The path climbs steadily and continues past the small towers supporting an inspection bridge at the start of the Blackton Reservoir. Oyster catchers and sandpipers call loudly as they fly along the edge of the wind stippled water. Fishermen stand placidly close to the shore, hoping to catch brown and rainbow trout.

Stroll along the path until you come to a large wrought-iron gate in the wall on the right. This gives access to a section of the Pennine Way and a view of Birk Hat, former home of Hannah Hauxwell, whose family farmed here for many years. Here a brood of redstarts plead to be fed and the adults flit from the fence to the ground and back with food. Walk to the stile in the wall to enjoy Hannah's Meadow Nature Reserve. These pastures were acquired in 1988 following Hannah's retirement from farming. The meadows are full of colour with globe flower, wood cranesbill, bugle, yellow rattle, pink clover and ragged robin.

Return to the large gate, and beyond turn right to walk the Pennine Way. Follow the waymarks as you pass below the huge dam of Balderhead Reservoir. Cross a bridge and follow the sign for the Pennine Way. Continue to a footbridge over a feeder stream and follow the signpost directions for the Bowes Loop of the Pennine Way and Clove Lodge.

Climb steadily uphill past more colourful hay meadows and through the gate beside Clove Lodge farm. Bear right onto a reinforced road and follow it as it swings left to cross Cotherstone Moor. Stride out along the lonely moorland road until you come to the signposted bridleway on the right. This leads over the moor to the slopes, and then the flat top, of Goldsborough. Enjoy the magnificent view and then descend its southern edge to pass along a thin track below the dramatic layered cliffs, used by novice climbers.

Follow the indistinct path (the Pennine Way) over the moor, where tormentil and bedstraw flower, to the edge of Yawd Sike. Drop down the slope and step across the sike. Climb up the opposite bank and, leaving the Pennine Way, make for the wall ahead. Follow it to the left, enjoying the wheatears and meadow pipits that use it to feed their young. Where the wall veers away to the right in the direction of a barn, a conifer plantation and a limekiln, continue ahead along the edge of a gill through which flows How Beck.

Walk along the rim of the gill - where grouse fly almost from under your feet and curlews call wildly from above as you come too close to their nest - until you see an ancient railway van on the opposite bank of the gill. Follow the clear path down the slope to a footbridge across How Beck. Continue downstream until you come to the delightful waterfall. Here the moorland stream, after hurrying between its steep grassy banks, descends with much grace and charm over stepped rocks into a deep narrow gorge. It drops in foaming tresses under rowan, willow, birch and wild rose. Overhead a heron flies low with a small bird trailing from its claws, mobbed by a frantic green plover.

Continue beside the glorious gill, with its magnificent layered sides, to a wide grassy track going off left, just before a ruined building. Follow it until you reach a road. Walk the road, and where it bears right take the signposted stile ahead. Walk down the slope to take a stile in the wall on the left beside an electricity pole. Walk ahead, keeping in line with the poles. Here several oyster catchers fly low over a flower filled ditch and a pair of redshanks tend their brood. Just before the wall ahead, turn right to pass through two gates of West Briscoe farm. Walk ahead to the road. Turn left and walk to the car park.

Hannah Hauxwell's old house

81

Waterfall close to Garrigill

18. Falls near Garrigill, High Pennines

GR 737424 (PF NY 64/74, 569 Alston), 4¹/₂ miles

G ARRIGILL WAS once a bustling mining centre and the village would have been noisy with the feet of lead miners, who wrested the ore from the layered and fissured limestone. It is a small, attractive village with stone houses bordering the large village green. Sit on the seat below one of two large limes that grace the green and enjoy the peace of this quiet hamlet set in a hollow in the moors.

Use the parking area, clearly marked, in front of the post office and near to the George and Dragon. Leave in the direction of Nenthead and Alston, crossing the bridge over the River South Tyne, which slides with much foam and noise over flat plates of limestone. Follow the flower bordered road as it swings left. To the left, and almost hidden by trees, the River South Tyne hurries northwards. At the junction continue in the direction of Alston and the imposing but decaying Methodist chapel, rebuilt in 1859. Look over the bridge that crosses the Garrigill Burn to see a man-made waterfall. here the tempestuous stream has been pleasingly channelled to drop many feet before passing beneath the stone arched bridge.

18. GARRIGILL

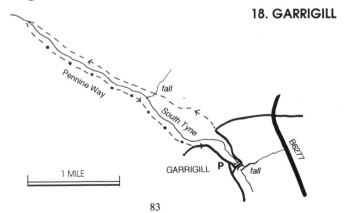

1 MILE

Step out along the road that passes through the quiet pastureland. Take the gated footpath, signposted Bleagate, on the left beyond the cemetery on the left. Once through the gate, bear right along the footpath to pass through an open gateway. Continue ahead, keeping the wall to the right. Ahead lies a small footbridge across a racing stream.

Before the bridge drop down the slope on the left, past a ruined limekiln. Farmers once burnt limestone in such kilns to produce lime to reduce the acidity of their pastures. A charming, easily-missed waterfall lies ahead. Here the small burn tumbles over limestone steps with ash, sycamore and elm casting their shade on the fall. Yellow hawkweed grows about the small amphitheatre of rock over which the skirt of water descends, brightening the hollow like a host of sunbeams. At the foot of the fall a deep pool has formed, from which the burn continues on its chattering way to join the River South Tyne.

Return and cross the footbridge. Walk the stiled way that keeps close to walled woodland and passes through

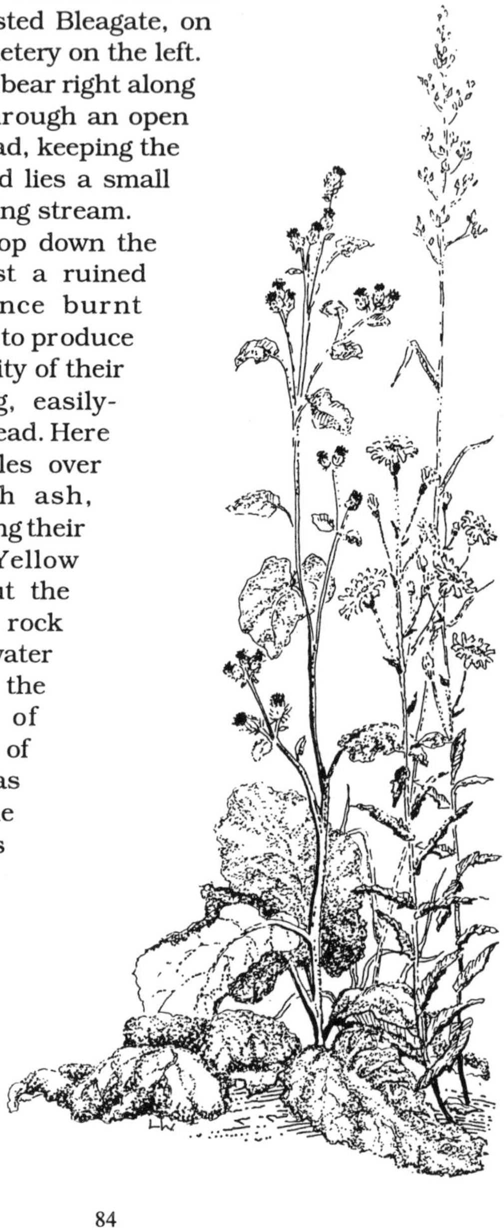

Burdock and hawkweed

84

fields full of summer flowers. To the left the trees drop down to the hurrying river. Pass to the right of Low Craig Farm and then bear left before walking ahead along a grassy track. In the trees beyond the wall a pair of redstarts scold angrily as the walkers' presence seems to threaten their brood.

Step out beside rowan, sycamore and larch until you reach Low Sillyhall, a derelict, deserted farmhouse with a poor stile to take you over the boundary wall. Walk ahead a few paces to pick up the Pennine Way and turn acute left. This well marked narrow path drops down below the tree covered slopes of the limestone scar over which you have just walked. The stiled way leads to the side of the River South Tyne. Bloody cranesbill, herb robert, pink campion and burdock line the path.

Cross the narrow footbridge over the river, just above some fast flowing rapids. Here along the banks grow large clumps of orange balsam. Follow the path upstream as it passes between scattered birch close to the water's edge. Enjoy this glorious flower-bedecked way, where pink orchis, wild thyme and dog roses grow. Look for the limekiln close to farm buildings.

A few yards upstream look for the pretty falls on the river where the South Tyne tumbles over a drop in its bed. A spotted flycatcher darts overhead after prey. Here in the grass grows the mauve and white mountain pansy.

Continue along the stiled way as the path, after passing scots pine and beech, climbs high above the gracious river and another attractive fall. Follow the Pennine Way signpost to the road. Turn left to walk past the Girls School built in 1850 and into Garrigill.

Nattrass Gill

19. Nattrass Gill, High Pennines

GR 719448, 4 miles

P ARK IN the centre of Alston, the highest market town in England. Walk down the splendid cobbled main street, past the Market Cross, where John Wesley once preached. Continue past St Augustine, the parish church of Alston. Turn left onto the A686 and walk towards the road bridge over the River South Tyne. Just before the bridge take the stepped Pennine Way on the left, which climbs steeply upwards, bordered with greater knotweed and figwort.

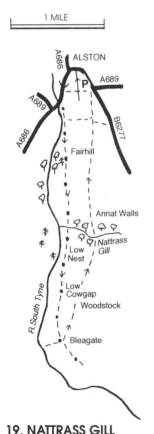

1 MILE

19. NATTRASS GILL

Follow the waymarked path to pass in front of the youth hostel, with a grand view down through mature trees to the river. This part of the walk is called The Firs and a plaque records that it is preserved for the people of Alston Moor.

The path continues beneath lofty beech and is littered with mast. Here grows wood cranesbill. Continue along the stiled way as the path moves away from the river with, ahead, a first view of Cross Fell. Cross the footbridge over the burn in Nattrass Gill and continue below a bank dotted with mauve and white mountain pansies. Walk on along the stiled way to pass close to Low Nest Farm and Low Cowgap Farm until you reach Bleagate Farm.

Pass through the waymarked stile beside the gate to walk between the farm buildings. Stride along the farm access road, a quiet way that is bordered with tall flowering grasses. Enjoy the view onto the lonely slopes of Alston Moor. Continue past Woodstock to where the road swings right. Here take the farm track on the left and then the footpath that leads off right - the signpost is obscured by a small sycamore tree. Cross the pasture, where swallows scream overhead, delirious with the super-abundance of flies, to a clearly waymarked stile.

Continue ahead into Nattrass Gill and descend the stepped (and slippery) way beneath beech, maple, hazel and ash. Cross a small footbridge and continue downward into this beautiful gill. A new footbridge takes you across the top of the charming waterfall. Here the burn drops, lace-like, in a skirt of white water, over a series of limestone ledges before racing onwards down the gill, its steep banks densely tree-clad; a yellow wagtail flies upstream; the sun streams through the tree trunks and the droplets from the fall sparkle and glisten - it is heaven indeed. That also is what the Victorians thought who often visited this lovely corner.

Continue up the steps beyond the bridge, remembering to look back for another view of the delightful fall. Step out into the pastures above to follow the waymarked posts to Annat Walls. Look for the dovecot on the right and the plaque over the house door which says "John and Sarah Friend 1735". Walk on past a barn with a perfect stone arch. It was once a dwelling. Continue along the farm track, which is bordered with mountain pansies, and past Fairhill Farm.

At the end of the track turn left and then almost immediately right into another. From this walled track you can hear curlews and redshanks calling. Where the way divides turn right to return to the main street. Turn left to walk over the cobbles to your car.

The dovecote

High Nent Head Force

20. Seven Sisters Waterfall and Nent Head Force, High Pennines

GRs 725468, 738469 (LR 87 Hexham & Haltwhistle, PF NY 64/74, 569 Alston), 3 miles

PARK IN the cobbled centre of Alston. Pass between the Crown Hotel and the Co-operative supermarket - just above the Market Cross - and drop down a walled footpath between buldings. Follow the path as it swings to the right and then climb the steps and cobbled way beyond, which is lined with herb robert, seeded grasses and wild raspberries. Look over the wall on the left to see a low white-painted house, built in 1747, with a crenellated stone porch. Overhead the air is filled with the excited screams of fly-hawking swifts.

Look for the footpath signposted Gossipgate beside the electricity sub-station. Walk ahead from the stile and bear left at the next signpost. Climb the waymarked stile and drop downhill diagonally right to another signposted stile in the wall. A charm of young goldfinches twitter noisily as they feed on sorrel and, when disturbed, fly off together.

Cross the next field, keeping to the right of the wall, and continue to Gossipgate Bridge. Look upstream to see the River Nent coming over in seven falls, each one passing through a deep fissure in the limestone and each one a lace-like flurry of white water. Along the banks grow harebells, buttercups, pink and white clover. Elms, sycamores, birch, hazel, and dog rose line the river bank. When you can tear yourself away from this glorious corner continue upstream.

Follow the footpath sign for Blagill Bridge. Climb the stile

20. SEVEN SISTERS WATERFALL AND NENT HEAD FORCE

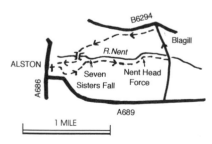

and look down onto the clints and grykes that for m the bed of the river. They are so regular in formation that they appear man-made. Look here for mountain pansies, with petals of pale and dark mauve. Walk on along the path, where meadow sweet, hawkweed, vetch, purple orchis and water avens create a magnificent floral garden.

Pass through a small alder copse where the lively river hurries below the path. Continue into a sun filled clearing wher e greater knapweed and wild mignonette flourish. Here too grow more pansies, some purple and white and others purple and yellow. Further along the path tall stemmed grass of par nassus grows.

Walk the stiled way into an alder wood. Suddenly thr ough the trees you have your first glimpse of Nent Head For ce, sometimes called Skelgill Force. Climb down to the riverside and, if the bur n is low, scramble along the r ocks to see the five foaming cascades of this lovely, elegant water fall. The white tresses descend into a very deep dark pool, its water swirling angrily at the base of the limestone amphitheatre of rock, eddying into small caves that earlier surges of water have for med. Spray fills the glorious hollow, over which hang elm, sycamore and ash.

Rejoin the path to climb the stile out of the wood. Look for the juicy bilberries that grow at the top of the fall. Pass thr ough a clearing and then into more woodland where the path climbs above the river. Leave the woodland by another stile and walk over the pastures beyond past orchis, ragged robin and the golden globeflower. Yellow balsam flowers in clumps along the river bank. Curlews and grouse call from the pastures beyond.

Climb the next stile to cross Blagill Bridge. Turn left and walk up the narrow lane, beside the Blagill Burn to Blagill village. Wander around this tiny settlement, which was built for lead miners and their families. One dwelling, now a far m, has a plaque with the date 1713 on it. Tur n left opposite the telephone box to pass some far m buildings and walk the unsignposted bridleway, keeping to the side of the wall on the right.

Continue ahead towards Corby Gates where, for a short distance, the path passes between walls beside a cr enellated outhouse. From one of the far m buildings led a tunnel, now blocked, which may have been used by the far mer and his family in ancient times to hide from marauding Scots. Follow the wall of the far m to the stile and beyond turn left. Follow the waymarks, keeping the wall to the right. Beyond the white metal gate drop down left through the pasture to a kissing gate in the wall ahead. Step out along the clear way to pass below Banks Farm.

Climb the next stile to walk a wide grassy walled track, which is lined with ash. This leads once more to the delightful arched Gossipgate Bridge. Cross the bridge and follow the track round, with the River Nent now on your right. Follow the track to enter Alston at the cobbled area known as the Butts and bear left to rejoin your car.

Grass of Parnassus

Ashgill Force

21. Ashgill Force, High Pennines

GR 759406, 4¹/₂ miles

P ARK IN the small village of Garrigill as for walk 18. Leave in the direction of Nenthead to cross the Garrigill Bridge. Look over the bridge to see the Straits of Garrigill - a narrow ravine in the river bed through which roars the confined River South Tyne. Walk ahead where the road swings left. Climb up the steep stony track beside a three storeyed building passing a modernised cottage that was built in 1661.

At the hilltop settlement of Loaning Head turn right to take the public footpath, signposted Pasture Houses. Walk ahead to a waymarked stile in the wall. The stiles crossed on this walk are exceedingly well built and easy to climb, and each step has been rounded for your boot to slip in comfortably. Each stile has a hand hold that has also been rounded and made smooth.

Continue past the ruined seventeenth-century farm of Windy Hall and then head for the far corner at the bottom of the pasture. Here a waymark on the telegraph pole directs you through a gate. Turn left and pass through farm buildings at Snappergill, where house martins glide overhead. Walk along a path to a gate onto an access track to the cottages at Pasture Houses. Cross, and take the stile ahead to walk in front of the former miners' cottages.

21. ASHGILL FORCE

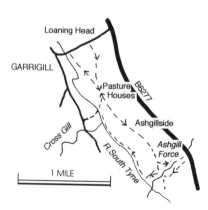

Continue onwards along the stiled way to a corrugated barn with a prominent waymark. Cross the stile to stand in front of the door of a dwelling with JRA 1734 inscribed on the lintel, in the hamlet of Ashgillside. Turn left, follow the track right looking for the

94

waymarked signpost ahead and climb two stiles. Turn right and walk to a gap in the wall. Turn left and walk ahead to the four-armed signpost by the footbridge at Ashgill.

Do not cross but follow the signpost directions for Ashgill Force. Walk along the steadily rising path through bracken and then trees, keeping close to the dancing river. A pair of grey wagtails flit from boulder to boulder as they head downstream to tend their brood. A first glimpse of the foot of the magnificent fall encourages you to hurry past some splendid cascades where the river descends a series of limestone steps. One more turn of the path and the magnificent fall lies ahead. Cross the stream on stepping stones, across the top of the highest of the cascades just passed, to obtain the best view of the grand waterfall.

The force comes under the road bridge (built in 1920) and then drops 40 to 50ft in long white ribbons of water into a hollow made quite dark by the huge amphitheatre of limestone. It finishes its descent in many lace-like cascades and then hurries down through the tree lined gill. Today only a wren and the chattering water disturb the peace of this lovely corner, but once it was filled with the noise and bustle of miners wresting the ore from the Ashgill Horse Level, now unsafe and gated. Return down the gill by the path that runs above the ruins of a mine building. Take the stile out of the woodland and continue along the path to a derelict building appropriately called Birds Nest, where a family of spotted flycatchers twitter from the branches of a dead elm.

Pass through the waymarked gate and drop downhill. This time cross the footbridge and follow the directions on the four-armed signpost for Low Crossgill. Look for the waterfall just below the bridge, where the water slides down a narrow funnel before being squeezed through an even narrower crevice to drop into a very deep dub. Walk on downstream beside this glorious burn as it flows through a deep ravine. Cross the waymarked stile to see the confluence of the Ashgill with the young River South Tyne. Bear right to walk beside the latter, where a dipper feeds.

The stiled path keeps beside the lovely tree-lined river. Continue past a bridge marked private and walk on beyond the junction of Cross Gill with the main river. Here the sheets of limestone forming the bed of the river are covered with the fallen petals of the many dog rose bushes that line its banks.

Pass through a kissing gate and walk down to Windshaw Bridge. Peer over to see the magnificent gorge below. Do not cross but take the waymarked stile to the right and climb the stepped way up through a plantation of Scots pine. Climb the stile out of the wood and follow the wall ahead uphill to a waymarked stile taken earlier.

"housemartins glide overhead"

Walk below Pasture Houses and ahead to the waymarked gate by the farm buildings at Snappergill. This time pass through the gate on the left and walk diagonally right across the pastures to the side the River South Tyne once more. Stride along the gated way to pass the Straits of Garrigill. At the bridge turn left and walk to the centre of the village.

Croglin Beck

22. Falls in Nunnery Walks, Eden Valley

GR 537424 (PF 44/54, 568 Southwaite & Kirkoswald), 4¹/₂ miles

START THE walk at Kirkoswald. Turn left out of its small square and walk uphill, using the cobbled pavement. Continue in the direction of Armathwaite, passing below a row of huge oaks. Beyond the last house of the village and the de-restriction sign, at the foot of a steep hill, take the footpath on the left, signposted Staffield. Walk along beside a small stream and turn right at the hedgerow to walk to a kissing gate.

Continue along the clear gated path to a stile that gives access to the parkland of Staffield Hall. The path is ill defined and you should walk ahead, bearing away to the left to a kissing gate close to the boundary wall of the hall. Continue beside the wall, and then the continuing fence, to a gate to rejoin the Armathwaite road. Turn left.

Stride out along the road past the hill on your left and descend beneath beech and birch trees to cross the Croglin Beck. Climb the hill beyond to the entrance to Nunnery House Hotel on the left.

The Nunnery House was rebuilt on the site of a Benedictine Convent in the early eighteenth century by Henry Aglionby. In 1752 Christopher Aglionby was born; he died, aged 33, in 1785. It was Christopher, in his short span of years, who laid out the magnificent Nunnery Walks. Wordsworth

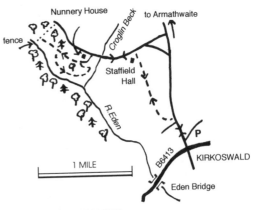

22. NUNNERY WALKS

98

wrote of their unrivalled beauty and in 1794 Hutchinson's *History of Cumberland* extolled their glory.

To enjoy this wonderful walk, pay the small entrance fee at the side door of the hotel and cross the lawn, following the arrowed notice. Follow the way as it swings to the right and then continues under limes and beech. Pass through the kissing gate and walk the high level path under an avenue of beech across parkland. Another kissing gate gives access to woodland and a board with a map. This shows the various paths, including those that require care.

And now the magical walk has really begun. Take the right fork where the path branches, following yellow waymarks. This passes through glorious deciduous woodland. After $1/4$ mile you can look down through the foliage to the white-topped rapids of the stately River Eden as it negotiates a drop in its bed. Here, on a boulder, a dipper bobs and curtseys. On the opposite bank huge red cliffs, almost covered with grey-green lichen, tower upwards supporting magnificent Scots pine. Look for the caves in the cliff face.

To the right of the path cliffs rear upwards covered with oaks and more Scots pine. Pass through a grassy area close to the grand river where the trees are waymarked and walk to the wire fence marking the end of the path. Return to the waymarked trees and take the right fork, which keeps close to the wide river.

Continue along the path where it has been hewn into the cliff. Huge sandstone overhangs, topped with trailing vegetation, shadow the ledge-like path. The river surges excitingly below and when in spate it turns the riverside way into a white-knuckle walk. This wonderful part of the walk should be taken slowly and savoured long.

Walk on to a rustic seat with an extensive view downstream. The path then comes to the confluence of the Croglin and the Eden and turns left, moving deep into woodland. A red squirrel races up an oak, its tail as long as its body. And then the deep, beautiful, savage gorge drops away to the right, with the mountain stream dancing merrily over its rocky bed. Ascend the stepped path that clings to the side of the ravine as it climbs high above the great chasm. Words cannot describe the spectacular view.

After more steps the path comes close to a summer-house. To reach the entrance take a short flight of steps on the right. Sit on

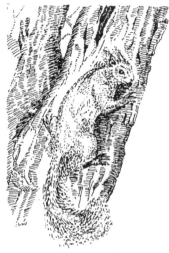

Red Squirrel

the seat and look at the fourteenth-century panels of coats of arms inset into the wall. These were probably parts of tombstones of the Aglionby family removed from St Cuthbert's Church, Carlisle, when it was demolished and rebuilt in 1778.

Walk on a short distance to a viewing platform to view the Croglin Beck waterfall as it gushes through parted rock to descend in a wall of white roaring foam. Return from the viewing platform and continue along the railed path on the edge of the gorge to another viewing area to see the waterfall in its entirety. The noise is tumultuous and the sight magnificent.

Return along the paths to the Nunnery House. Retrace your outward route, past Staffield House and over the pastures to Kirkoswald.

Near Cotherstone

23. Cotherstone to falls on the River Tees and on a small feeder stream

GR 040175, 025195, 6¹/₂ miles

THE ATTRACTIVE village of Cotherstone lies to the south of the River Tees and 3 miles north-west of Barnard Castle. Formerly a purely agricultural community it grew with the coming of Tees Valley Railway in the nineteenth century. The railway closed in 1964 and the village has expanded little since. In the 1980s it gained fame from being the retirement home of Hannah Hauxwell.

Start your walk from a parking area in front of the Fox and Hounds on West Green. Walk along the main street of the linear village, past the post office and Hannah's house, to East Green. Stand on the little bridge over the beck to see the fine spire of St Cuthbert's church - a spire is a rare sight in Teesdale. Follow the signpost directions at East Green to visit the Quaker Meeting House, built in 1797. The signpost directs you along a ginnel (a path between houses) across a back lane and then through a gate to take the path to the church. Sit on one of the bench seats and enjoy the peace of the walled burial ground, which is edged with lofty larch and Scots pine. Continue along the stiled path to pass two small ponds with ducks, moorhens, a heron and a clump of magnificent bullrushes. The ponds were reclaimed from a boggy area, part of a conservation project by the village.

Walk on to a bridge over a stream and take the waymarked path to climb uphill to a stile. Keep left over two fields to a stile in a wall. Keep straight ahead to follow the waymarked edge of glorious woodland with oaks and hazel clad in lemon coloured leaves which brighten a late October day. Pass through a waymarked gate and continue ahead along a grassy track close to farm buildings, to an arrow pointing left to the River Tees. Here turn right to walk through two gates enclosing the outbuildings of Cooper House (1722). Walk ahead, keeping the wood to your left. Look over the wall to see the stately Tees far below.

Continue beside the walled wood, following the waymarked stiled way. Stride the clear path across a pasture to where the path divides into three. Take the middle path leading to a stream crossed by a clapper bridge. (Try to decipher the date carved in the stone slab.) The narrow path leads into Towlerhill Plantation where fly agaric toadstools grow beneath birch. Follow the clearly defined path through the trees to exit to a pasture. Continue left to cross the pasture to the right of a finger of woodland (waymarked).

Stride on in the same direction, keeping Towlerhill Wood away to the left. On reaching the boundary wall ahead turn right to walk beside it to join a waymarked track which leads towards the farm of Towler Hill. Carry on along the track as it turns right and 100yds along look for the waymarked stile on the left. Head on along the path, keeping to the left of the hawthorn hedge to a stile in the corner. Continue across the corner of a pasture to an arrowed stile to cross the dismantled railway.

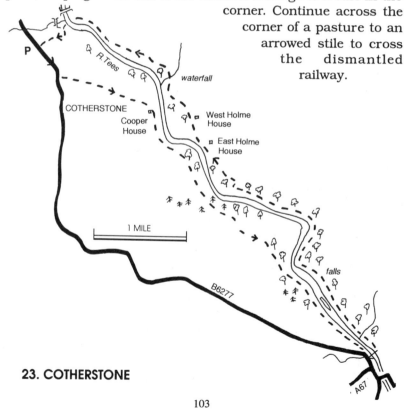

23. COTHERSTONE

Follow the path through the riotously coloured woodland, where jays call raucously. Descend the steps in the shadow of the remains of the once magnificent viaduct that spanned the Tees. What a sight it must have been. One of the reasons given for removing it was safety: Barnard Castle boys weren't considered men until they had crossed the viaduct by using the ledge on the outside of the bridge!

Continue along the way where the path joins a cart-track and walk on along it to the gate onto the B6277. Turn left and take the footpath, left, to cross the portalled Deepdale Aqueduct. Look south-east for a grand view of the castle. At the far side of the bridge, turn left and follow the waymarks to cross a footbridge that leads to a spacious picnic area by the side of the river. Sit here and listen for the shrill whistle of a kingfisher and then watch it fly rapidly upstream. Its bright blue metallic colouring, sometimes flashing brilliant green depending on the rays of light, makes this a magic moment.

Walk on along the good footpath, keeping within sight and sound of the magnificent Tees. Pass through beech, rowan, oak, ash and birch now garbed in the reds, yellows and gold of autumn. Continue beneath vertical sandsone cliffs, well wooded, with frequent stretches of white water below. Pass beneath the derelict buttress of the viaduct. Look for one of the aims of the walk, the white-topped falls where the mature Tees is squeezed through a narrow gap in the rock plates of its bed. It foams, roars and sprays, showing much youthful vigour. Fortunately several trees have been felled and the view of the fall is unobscured.

Watch for grey squirrels hunting for acorns below oaks and for redwings chattering in the tree tops. Take care along the path where it becomes muddy and where there is a steep drop beside the path down to the deep surging water.

Pass through the gate that gives access to a pasture and then take the waymarked gate in the wall, 20yds on your right. Beyond, climb the steep muddy path to the top edge of the wood. Turn left and walk the stiled way to pass East Holme House, keeping the lovely woodland to your left. Continue the well marked way to pass in front of West Holme House and on to a stile into a wooded gill. The stile has a considerable drop on the far side so take care. Follow the path downhill to a clapper bridge. To the left lies the small but bonny waterfall, that is the second aim of the walk. The hurrying stream tumbles over layered ledges of rock into a dark pool. Sycamores shed their yellow leaves and these fall into the pool and are carried by the beck on its way to add its water to the Tees.

Climb the stile on the far side of the clapper bridge and walk uphill with the wall to your left. Pass through a gate in the wall (waymark on far side!) and strike left across the pasture to walk the gated way beside the lovely woodland once more. Look for the stepped stile beside a sheep hurdle into the wood and follow the path down through the trees to continue across a pasture to the footbridge over the river. As you cross look for a dipper running into the shallows after prey. Turn left on the far side and follow the path to cross the footbridge over the River Balder. Pause by the picnic table to enjoy this glorious confluence of two splendid rivers.

Ascend the path opposite the footbridge (63 steps) to a stile on top of Hallgarth Hill, and walk along the narrow lane. To the right is the site of a twelfth-century castle, the home of the medieval lords of Cotherstone, the Fitzhughs. Walk on to look down on the Hagg, a public open space that used to be common pasture. Continue to the main street, opposite the Fox and Hounds and your car.

Fly agaric

Rutter Force

24. Rutter Force, near Appleby

GR 682158 (PF NY 61/71, 597 Crosby Ravensworth & Brough), 8 miles

A PPLEBY-IN-WESTMORLAND LIES in the glorious Eden valley, where it skirts the foot of the Pennines. Park close to Appleby Castle at the top of Bor oughgate. Walk out of the town, keeping the castle wall to your left, along Shaws W iend. Cross the road and take the signposted right tur n towards Colby to walk 20yds into Colby Lane. Take the footpath on the left, signposted Bandley Bridge. Walk ahead to a ladder stile, then to a stile in the left corner of the next pastur e, which leads to a grassy lane. Tur n right and almost immediately take a stile on your left.

Walk ahead, with a fence and then a hedge to the left. Climb the stile in the left corner to turn right onto an unsurfaced lane. 50yds along look for the waymarked footpath sign (green arrow) on your left. Walk along the field edge to pass through a painted white stile to take a similar one on the right. Bear right across the field to another white-topped stile. Drop down the long pasture to a wall stile on the right which gives access to a footbridge over the Hoff Beck.

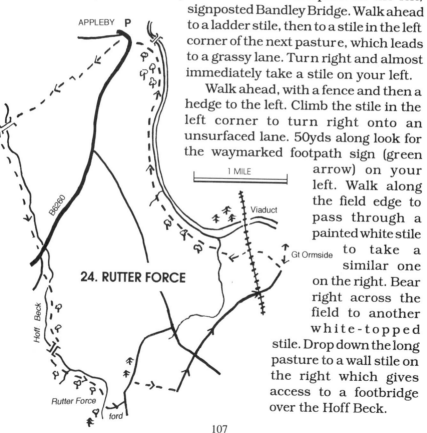

APPLEBY · P

1 MILE

B6260

Viaduct

Gt Ormside

24. RUTTER FORCE

Hoff Beck

Rutter Force

ford

107

Turn left and take the bridleway (blue arrow) to walk beside the sparkling stream, silvery in the winter sunshine. Continue through a hazel copse where a host of redwings feed ravenously on the berries of nearby hawthorns. Keep to the path to the left of the track as it begins to climb, to take the stile marked with a green arrow and continue beside the Hoff.

Stroll beside the stream to cross several stiles beside the water. Long tailed tits flit excitedly through alders, unconcerned by a pair of buzzards overhead. On the edge of the village of Hoff, take an unmarked gate on the right, just beyond the first barn, to walk to a waymarked gate ahead that directs you to the B6260 and the New Inn. Cross the road and walk the narrow road, signposted Drybeck and Oakbeck, with the Hoff flowing to your left.

Turn left into an unmarked farm track and walk to a gate. Beyond, cross a new footbridge over the Hoff. Turn right and walk upstream. Fieldfares call raucously from trees overhead. Keep close to the beck to pass through a gate and then a broken stile. The next stile is awkward to cross, but find the easiest way over and continue to another new footbridge with a sturdy stile. Beyond, turn left and continue upstream to another good stile. Here you have your first spectacular sighting of Rutter Force. Hurry ahead across a field to a gate to the narrow road and the former cornmill, now a small tearoom and coffee shop.

Walk left to stand on the footbridge over the Hoff to view the magnificent Rutter Force, which flows with great noise and power. Its waters then lose their fury and continue placidly over a ford, much to the delight of innumerable ducks. Continue up the narrow lane to turn left onto Broadmire Road.

After 200yds, take the stiled footpath, signposted Ormside, on the right. It leads to pastures from which there is a wonderful view of the High Pennines, from Cross Fell to Long Fell. At the lane, turn left and walk ahead for a mile to Great Ormside, with another dramatic view of the fells to encourage you on your way.

Look for the old AA sign on a wall on the left in the village, which says it is 273 miles to London. Notice the signposted footpath to Appleby. This is the path to take after visiting the church at the far end of the village. As you walk towards St James's you pass beneath a huge sycamore growing out of massive steps. This is believed to have been planted in 1693 to replace the old market cross, probably destroyed during the Civil War. A cheese and butter market was held here until recent times.

Walk on to visit the church, one of the oldest in the diocese of Carlisle. A former priest, John de Grote, drafted the will of the Black Prince in 1376, and a copy is on view. The church is built on a defensive mound, overlooking the River Eden. Inside look for the Norman arches and the Norman bowl of the font. Outside, from the base of the sturdy Norman tower, you can glimpse the river and the sandstone viaduct spanning it. As you leave the church notice Ormside Hall, which has a late fourteenth-century pele tower.

Leave this lovely corner and return to the footpath to Appleby, now on your right. The waymarked route is very clear and takes you under a bridge carrying the Settle to Carlisle railway. Beyond, follow the footpath sign that directs you to Appleby via the River Eden. A wide grassy way swings left and then you walk right at the end of the track. Here cross a small plank footbridge over a ditch on your right and take the stile on your right into the woodland of Jeremy Gill. From now on the path continues ahead, well waymarked through splendid deciduous woodland and coming close to the River Eden. Suddenly you have a splendid view of the tower of Appleby Castle.

Continue along the stiled and gated way, with the Eden to your right. No directions required, but look for bullfinches and dippers. When you are confronted by two stiles take the one on the left and walk to a kissing gate onto a road. Turn left and walk beside the castle wall. Continue along Scattergate and then Shaws Wiend and Boroughgate to regain your car.

Ormside Hall

The second fall in Hamsterley Forest

25. Falls in Hamsterley Forest
GRs 054275, 057278, 1 mile

HAMSTERLEY FOREST, owned by the Forestry Commission, covers 5,000 acres. It lies north-east of Middleton-in-Teesdale, which you leave by the B6282. After 8 miles, just before the village of Woodland, turn left, following the signboard for the forest. Take the next left, pass close to Coal Board buildings and drive along the single-track road into woodland. Continue to the bridge over the Spurlswood Beck and park in the large clearing on the right, beyond the stream.

Walk back to the bridge, but do not cross, and take the waymarked path on the left. Look for the delightful water fall below the bridge. The beck races over a series of ledges, white and foaming and deeply stained with peat, to fall into a dark pool. Oak, silver birch and ash lean over the hollow. Their pale lemon leaves drop to the water and then drift gently downstream. The morning sun dispels the last of the November mist and highlights the autumn tints.

Continue along the steadily climbing path, which is littered with beech leaves, bronzed and curled. Cross a small stream on convenient stones and walk ahead through a planting of tall larch. Beyond these the path levels out and passes through young larch, dressed in soft lemon needles and festooned with silvery cobwebs. From away to the left comes the harsh chattering of a sparrowhawk.

Follow the narrow path as it drops down the slope to the edge of a forest track. Turn right and walk to the first bridge over the beck. Beyond take the waymarked steps on the left and follow the path through

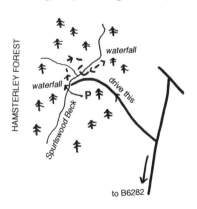

25. HAMSTERLEY FOREST

111

the glorious woodland, keeping close to the tumbling stream. Goldcrests whisper quietly in the conifers and toadstools grow beside the path.

Look for the spindle-shaped cones gnawed by squirrels and then discarded on the footpath.

Where the footpath divides, keep to the branch beside the stream to cross a small footbridge. Beyond lies the waterfall. The beck descends in a peat-stained cascade over a low amphitheatre of rock into a very deep dark basin before hurrying on past beech and birch. A branch of birch has fallen over the top of the fall and its small twigs are encased in ice and icicles hang from the larger branches.

Return along the path to the steps and then continue left along the forest track. This joins the track that leads to the bridge and the parking area lies beyond.

Fall in Hamsterley Forest
113

26. Fall in Hamsterley Forest

GR 037293, 6 miles

P ARK AT the Grove parking area, which is approached from Windy Bank Road, west of Hamsterley. The access road is lined with deciduous and coniferous trees, riotously coloured in November. Follow the red arrow waymarks, for the High Acton walk, out of the car park. Climb the steps beneath a lofty monkey puzzle tree and continue along the narrow path to the forest road. Notice this unmarked point as this is the route to return.

Cross the road and follow the path downhill to join another forest track. Turn left to cross a bridge over the Euden Beck and continue between buildings used as a forestry training centre. From the conifers on the right jays screech raucously in loud contrast to the whispers of coal tits close by the track. To the left, beyond the beck, the steep slopes support many young larch, all clad in pale lemon needles which catch the thin wintry sun.

Stroll the easy-to-walk way, keeping close to the hurrying Euden, a joyful narrow beck that tumbles in many falls as it hurries through the gill. Enjoy also the falls on the narrow streams that hurry down the slopes on the right, between the tall conifers. Notice the small boxes placed high on tree trunks to encourage bats. Follow the track for 1 1/2 miles and then as it drops into a hollow. Look left, beyond the Euden, to a beck descending in elegant, lace-like curtains of water from conifers high on rocky

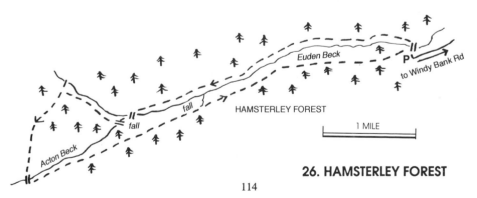

26. HAMSTERLEY FOREST

114

slopes. The cascades pass through willow, still supporting some yellowy-green leaves, before plummeting into the Euden.

Continue along the track, crossing the Euden by a small bridge, and then climb the slope beyond. At the branching of the track, take the left fork and continue ascending. Look left through the conifers to see another pleasing fall. Follow the waymarks directing you left through the trees to walk a wide path which is heavily carpeted with needles. These deaden the sound of your footsteps and are soft to walk on after the hardened surfaces of the forest tracks.

Jays screech raucously

The wide path comes to a wooden footbridge and then a row of steps, which you ascend. Head on until you reach some duckboarding. Walk along this as it swings left and right. The path continues through the trees and leads you to a forest track and the sunlight. Turn left. After 50yds turn left again to walk another forest track, high above the Acton Beck.

This is a grand track. The dark firs soon give way, on the right, to larch covered with saffron needles which drop continually. Young coal tits flit across the track, seemingly as light and delicate as the needles. Then the forest opens out and to the left the land drops steeply down to the Euden. The young larch seen earlier cover the slope and contrast attractively with the dark needled firs far below. Ahead lies the extensive grouse moor of Hamsterley Common.

At a junction of tracks, walk on a dozen yards to find the narrow path on the right that leads down the slope, below the monkey puzzle tree, to the car park.

115

Fall on the Tees

27. River Tees and Sledwich Gill near Barnard Castle

GRs 052159, 093146, 9 miles

B ARNARD CASTLE in December welcomes visitors with fairy lights, gaily decked shops, a crib and a silver band composed of young teenagers playing carols. It makes a cheery start to a splendid pre-Christmas walk.

Park in the large free car park off Galgate, a wide street lined with trees and shops. Return to Galgate, cross the road and walk left to the post office, a large white building on the corner of the street. Cross the road ahead and continue beside Trinity Methodist Church to a waymarked walks information board. Pause here to enjoy a grand view of the twelfth-century castle, with its glorious round tower. Turn right to walk a tarmac path between a children's paddling pool and swings.

Continue down the path to where it meets the River Tees in Flatts Wood. Cross the Tees Aqueduct bridge, from where you have good views, left, of the castle and, right, of the buttresses of the Old Tees Valley viaduct seen on walk 23. Join the Middleton-in-Teesdale road and turn left into Flax Field. Walk past the site of Ullathorne's Mill, built in 1798, where once shoe thread and twine were produced.

Pass County Bridge on your left (do not cross) and walk on along The Sills, a quiet road on the west bank of the alder lined Tees. Continue until you reach the footpath sign to Egglestone Abbey, on the left, just where the Tees makes a wide swing to the east. Look left to see the Thorngate footbridge over the hurrying water.

Keep to the footpath close to the Tees, which is now edged with ash trees bearing large bunches of brown seed keys. Look for the pleasing falls where the deep water, stained with peat, descends in white topped cascades over a very long, sideways facing fault in the stepped rock of the river bed. The sun catches the surging water as it noisily descends.

After enjoying the attractive fall return to Thorngate footbridge

117

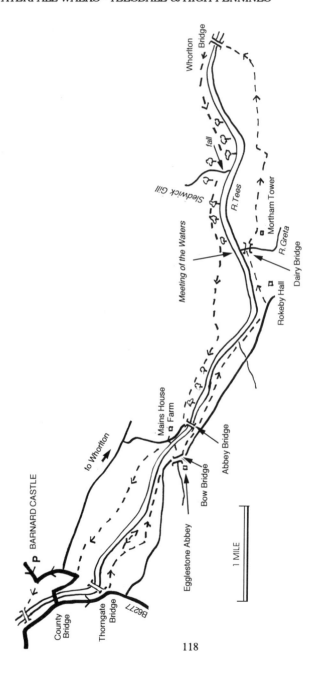

27. RIVER TEES AND SLEDWICH GILL

1 MILE

118

and turn left to climb a steep railed path. Turn left at the top and walk along a path and road to a gated stile into a caravan site. Turn right to walk uphill along a tarmac road to take a waymarked stile on the left. From here enjoy your first view of Bowes Museum, designed in the style of a French chateau and set in rural surroundings, and Barnard Castle School. Walk ahead from the stile for a pleasing high level walk through four fields, with the Tees far below to your left.

Pass through the gap stile to Abbey Lane, turn left and walk downhill to the bridge over Thorsgill Beck in the shadow of the ruins of Egglestone Abbey. Look over the bridge to see the seventeenth-century packhorse bridge alongside. Continue, and take the access road on the right to the Abbey, which was founded by Ralph de Multon in 1195. Pass through the kissing gate and wander through the picturesque ruins. Enjoy the impressive view of the river far below.

Return to Abbey Lane and walk on for ¹/₄ mile to Abbey Bridge. This former toll-bridge, built in 1773, is 60ft high. Stand on the bridge and enjoy the glorious views of the tree-lined gorge, through which the river rages over many stepped, horizontal layers of limestone. A goosander duck, with long narrow beak and cigar-shaped body, swims serenely through the peaceful shallows.

Continue beside the Tees, remaining on the south bank. A signpost to the Meeting of the Waters directs you into woodland for a delightful walk, often called "Paradise Walk", beside the stately Tees. Climb the stile, cross the stepping stones and ascend the steps of Manyfold Gill to walk above the Tees. The river, now out of its gorge, flows noisily.

As the way comes nearer to the water look for dippers courting - bowing, posturing and showing off their white bibs. Take the waymarked stile into woodland, where marsh tits slip through the branches calling "cheevi, cheevi, cheevi". Follow the path as it swings right to pass through ash and beech to a gate to Mortham Lane. Turn left and continue ahead, with the Tees below to the left. On the right stands Rokeby Hall, where Sir Walter Scott stayed while writing his poetry. Continue ahead to the Meeting of the Waters. Here the River Greta pours its water, over a litter of huge boulders, into the Tees. Many long tailed tits excitedly hunt for prey over-wintering in the nuts of an alder that shadows the confluence.

Continue along the way to cross Dairy Bridge, which spans the dark rocky gorge through which the tempestuous River Greta hastens. Stride on along a driveway to Mortham Tower, a manor house with pele tower (not open to the public). Where you come level with the tower, look left to see the waymarked stile. Beyond, walk ahead, keeping close to a thorn hedge where dozens of redwings feast on the plenteous haws. To the left the cliffs of the far bank of the Tees turn yellow in the sunlight and the river is a wide band of blue. Pass through two stiles and then keep close beside woodland on the left.

Follow the path as it swings left on the outside of the trees and then turn right to walk to the right of a wall. Pass a roofless farm building and through a gap in the corner of the pasture to walk ahead. Look for goldfinches in the burdocks to the side of the waymarked gate ahead. Beyond, strike diagonally left to a stone stile to the road and a suspension bridge, Whorlton Bridge - 32ft high. From the bridge look downstream to see more dramatic falls where great stepped plates of limestone, sideways on, cause the Tees to foam and fall in pleasing cascades.

Pass the old toll cottage on the far side of the bridge and then climb signposted steps on the left. Near the top is a well-placed seat. Sit here and enjoy the nuthatches hunting for insects in the crevices of bark. Continue up to the road. Turn left and walk a few yards to the signposted footpath that runs along the wooded Whorlton Bank, high above the Tees. Beyond the kissing gate continue along the stiled and gated waymarked path, keeping the wood to the left. Follow a waymark to descend steep steps into Sledwich Gill. At the bottom of the steps, cross the beck just above a pretty waterfall. Here the stream plummets white-topped over a steep stepped drop in its bed. It then tumbles on through the narrow gill to join the Tees, overshadowed by sheer golden cliffs. Trees grow where they can obtain a hold and the gill is choked with vegetation.

Climb out of the gill to a stone stile in the cross wall. Beyond, look for the Dorset Horn ram with his ewes and lambs. Continue along the stiled way high above the river gorge. Beyond the stile, at the end of the trees on the left, walk ahead to straddle the damaged stone stile almost in the right corner of the pasture. Then strike half left across the field to another stone stile. Aim for a wooden stile close to Tees Bank Plantation on the left. Proceed over three more pastures, climbing a wooden fence each time. Pass through a gate in the hedge ahead and continue beside a wall. Look left to see Abbey Bridge.

Keep to the wall side and look for the gated gap stile near the far corner. This gives access to the road. Turn right and walk ahead to the bend. Take the waymarked gate on the left heading towards the museum. From this path there is a good view of Egglestone Abbey. It is probably the place where Turner sat to paint his view of the abbey. Continue along the stile and waymarked route, still well above the Tees. Follow the distinct grassy path as it swings diagonally right across The Demesne - this is the area, in past centuries, that the lord of the manor allowed the people, who worked at the castle, to cultivate.

Walk ahead to a kissing gate and follow the track that swings right. Pass through Broadgate, an alleyway that leads into The Bank. Turn right to pass the Market Cross, the crib, the streets and the shops illuminated with Christmas lights.

Mill Force

28. Mill Force, Bowes

GRs 993134, 976125, 8 miles

PARK IN the centre of Bowes, opposite the post office, where there are several large bays for cars. Walk west along the main street to pass St Giles's church and turn left beyond, along Beck Street, to the entrance to Bowes Castle.

The ruined castle and the church occupy the site of the northern part of a Roman fort which was nearly square with rounded corners. The castle dates from the twelfth century and was built for Henry II. Scottish invaders besieged it in the same century and again in the fourteenth, when Robert the Bruce laid it waste.

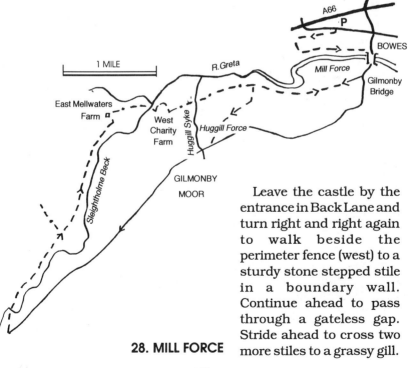

28. MILL FORCE

Leave the castle by the entrance in Back Lane and turn right and right again to walk beside the perimeter fence (west) to a sturdy stone stepped stile in a boundary wall. Continue ahead to pass through a gateless gap. Stride ahead to cross two more stiles to a grassy gill.

Turn left and walk downhill to the side of the wide surging River Greta. Turn left and climb the stile into deciduous woodland.

Follow the good path through the trees from where you can see the dramatic Mill Force below. Pass out of the wood by a stile and walk down to the riverside for a pleasing view of the hurrying Greta. Its silvery water descends huge rocky plates in the river bed throwing up white-topped foam laced with rich orange-brown from the peat gathered on its journey through the moors. Masonry about the river bank and stone piles in the water remind you that once the energy of the fast-flowing river was put to good use.

Continue along the stiled way beside the river to Gilmonby Bridge, where you turn right and walk into the small settlement of the same name. Stride past the post box and take the next right turn, signposted West Gates and Lady Myres. Enjoy the narrow lane that takes you through the quiet pastures below Gilmonby Moor, past warm brownstone houses, walls and barns.

Pass West Gates and West Pasture farms and take the tied gate on the left, beyond the next wall. Stride ahead to pass through the next gate. Turn right to walk to the gate in the wall ahead. Beyond, turn left to climb uphill, with a wall to your left. (The right of way crosses diagonally, but the stone stepped stile in the far right corner has disappeared.)

Go through the gate to join a grassy track leading up over rough fell to a gate to a moorland road. To the right of the grassy track a small moorland stream, the Huggill, impetuously descends a steep fault in its bed. It first drops over a small ledge and then plummets in a glorious lace-like cascade to a dark hollow in the gill. Grassy slopes enclose the tiny beck and rowans grow along its banks. Huggill Force is a very bonny waterfall.

Beyond the gate to the moorland road, turn right to walk 1 1/2 miles along the lonely way over Gilmonby Moor. On a raw December day grouse seem to be your only companions - and even they tell you to "go back, go back". Pass Bar Gap farm and descend the road beyond to take a poorly waymarked gate (part of the Pennine Way) beyond a barn on the right. Walk diagonally right to pass through a gate and continue to cross the gated Intake footbridge, over Sleightholme Beck, towards the right end of Bog Scar.

Walk the upper path, that climbs right up the slope, to follow the

St Giles' Church, Bowes

path close to the wall on your left. Follow the path thr ough gates to pass to the left of Trough Heads farm. Do not follow the Pennine Way, which leads off left. Continue ahead along the stiled way and where the path comes close to a wall to your right look over into the delightful wooded gorge through which races the beck.

At the end of the gorge take the left of two gates and follow the wall on your right to a stepped stile that is easy to miss. Strike diagonally left across the large pasture to a stile in the wall to the right of East Mellwaters farm. This leads you into a small conifer plantation where you turn left to struggle through low branches to a gate. From the gate continue ahead to another, on your left, which is on the right side of the far m. Turn right, walk beside the farm and turn right through a waymarked gate beyond the far m and between outbuildings. You have now rejoined the Pennine Way.

Continue ahead, passing through the left of two gates - that is, the gate nearest to the River Greta. (This gate also is easy to miss.) The way now continues between the wall on your right and the surging water to your left. Follow the wall r ound to cross the waymarked Cardwell Bridge, recrossing Sleightholme Beck just before its union with the Greta.

Beyond the bridge, turn left to West Charity Farm, where you see your first Pennine Way signpost. Follow the farm track, right, along the far side of the farm, and beyond a gate turn left as directed by another signpost. Walk the lane to cross the lower end of Huggill beck and continue to Lady Myres farm. Beyond, the Pennine Way crosses the Greta but the stepping stones are often under water and there is no bridge.

Continue along the lane until you reach Gilmonby, where you turn left to cross the bridge over the river. Follow the lane uphill to return to your car.

CICERONE GUIDES
Cicerone publish a wide range of reliable guides to walking and climbing in Britain, and other general interest books.

LAKE DISTRICT - General Books
CONISTON COPPER A History
CHRONICLES OF MILNTHORPE
A DREAM OF EDEN
THE HIGH FELLS OF LAKELAND
LAKELAND - A taste to remember (Recipes)
LAKELAND VILLAGES
LAKELAND TOWNS
THE LOST RESORT? (Morecambe)
LOST LANCASHIRE (Furness area)
OUR CUMBRIA Stories of Cumbrian Men and Women
THE PRIORY OF CARTMEL
REFLECTIONS ON THE LAKES
AN ILLUSTRATED COMPANION INTO LAKELAND

LAKE DISTRICT - Guide Books
THE BORDERS OF LAKELAND
BIRDS OF MORECAMBE BAY
CASTLES IN CUMBRIA
CONISTON COPPER MINES Field Guide
THE CUMBRIA CYCLE WAY
THE EDEN WAY
IN SEARCH OF WESTMORLAND
SHORT WALKS IN LAKELND-1: SOUTH LAKELAND
SCRAMBLES IN THE LAKE DISTRICT
MORE SCRAMBLES IN THE LAKE DISTRICT
WALKING ROUND THE LAKES
WALKS IN SILVERDALE/ARNSIDE
WESTMORLAND HERITAGE WALK
WINTER CLIMBS IN THE LAKE DISTRICT

NORTHERN ENGLAND (outside the Lakes
BIRDWATCHING ON MERSEYSIDE
CANAL WALKS Vol 1 North
CANOEISTS GUIDE TO THE NORTH EAST
THE CLEVELAND WAY & MISSING LINK
THE DALES WAY
DOUGLAS VALLEY WAY
WALKING IN THE FOREST OF BOWLAND
HADRIANS WALL Vol 1 The Wall Walk
HERITAGE TRAILS IN NW ENGLAND
THE ISLE OF MAN COASTAL PATH
IVORY TOWERS & DRESSED STONES (Follies)
THE LANCASTER CANAL
LANCASTER CANAL WALKS
A WALKERS GUIDE TO THE LANCASTER CANAL
LAUGHS ALONG THE PENNINE WAY
A NORTHERN COAST-TO-COAST
NORTH YORK MOORS Walks
THE REIVERS WAY (Northumberland)
THE RIBBLE WAY
ROCK CLIMBS LANCASHIRE & NW
WALKING DOWN THE LUNE
WALKING IN THE SOUTH PENNINES
WALKING IN THE NORTH PENNINES
WALKING IN THE WOLDS
WALKS IN THE YORKSHIRE DALES (3 VOL)
WALKS IN LANCASHIRE WITCH COUNTRY
WALKS IN THE NORTH YORK MOORS
WALKS TO YORKSHIRE WATERFALLS (2 vol)
WATERFALL WALKS -TEESDALE & THE HIGH PENNINES
WALKS ON THE WEST PENNINE MOORS
WALKING NORTHERN RAILWAYS (2 vol)
THE YORKSHIRE DALES A walker's guide

Also a full range of EUROPEAN and OVERSEAS guidebooks - walking, long distance trails, scrambling, ice-climbing, rock climbing.

DERBYSHIRE & EAST MIDLANDS
KINDER LOG
HIGH PEAK WALKS
WHITE PEAK WAY
WHITE PEAK WALKS - 2 Vols
WEEKEND WALKS IN THE PEAK DISTRICT
THE VIKING WAY
THE DEVIL'S MILL / WHISTLING CLOUGH (Novels)

WALES & WEST MIDLANDS
ASCENT OF SNOWDON
WALKING IN CHESHIRE
CLWYD ROCK
HEREFORD & THE WYE VALLEY A Walker's Guide
HILLWALKING IN SNOWDONIA
HILL WALKING IN WALES (2 Vols)
THE MOUNTAINS OF ENGLAND & WALES Vol 1 WALES
WALKING OFFA'S DYKE PATH
THE RIDGES OF SNOWDONIA
ROCK CLIMBS IN WEST MIDLANDS
SARN HELEN Walking Roman Road
SCRAMBLES IN SNOWDONIA
SNOWDONIA WHITE WATER SEA & SURF
THE SHROPSHIRE HILLS A Walker's Guide
WALKING DOWN THE WYE
WELSH WINTER CLIMBS

SOUTH & SOUTH WEST ENGLAND
WALKING IN THE CHILTERNS
COTSWOLD WAY
COTSWOLD WALKS (3 VOLS)
WALKING ON DARTMOOR
WALKERS GUIDE TO DARTMOOR PUBS
EXMOOR & THE QUANTOCKS
THE KENNET & AVON WALK
LONDON THEME WALKS
AN OXBRIDGE WALK
A SOUTHERN COUNTIES BIKE GUIDE
THE SOUTHERN-COAST-TO-COAST
SOUTH DOWNS WAY & DOWNS LINK
SOUTH WEST WAY - 2 Vol
THE TWO MOORS WAY Dartmoor-Exmoor
WALKS IN KENT Bk 2
THE WEALDWAY & VANGUARD WAY

SCOTLAND
THE BORDER COUNTRY - WALKERS GUIDE
BORDER PUBS & INNS A Walker's Guide
CAIRNGORMS WINTER CLIMBS
WALKING THE GALLOWAY HILLS
THE ISLAND OF RHUM
THE SCOTTISH GLENS (Mountainbike Guide)
    Book 1:THE CAIRNGORM GLENS
    Book 2 THE ATHOLL GLENS
    Book 3 THE GLENS OF RANNOCH
SCOTTISH RAILWAY WALKS
SCRAMBLES IN LOCHABER
SCRAMBLES IN SKYE
SKI TOURING IN SCOTLAND
TORRIDON A Walker's Guide
WALKS from the WEST HIGHLAND RAILWAY
WINTER CLIMBS BEN NEVIS & GLENCOE

REGIONAL BOOKS UK & IRELAND
THE ALTERNATIVE PENNINE WAY
CANAL WALKS Vol.1: North
LIMESTONE - 100 BEST CLIMBS
THE PACKHORSE BRIDGES OF ENGLAND
THE RELATIVE HILLS OF BRITAIN
THE MOUNTAINS OF ENGLAND & WALES
    VOL 1 WALES, VOL 2 ENGLAND
THE MOUNTAINS OF IRELAND

Other guides are constantly being added to the Cicerone List.
Available from bookshops, outdoor equipment shops or direct (send s.a.e. for price list) from
CICERONE, 2 POLICE SQUARE, MILNTHORPE, CUMBRIA, LA7 7PY

Text printed by St Edmundsbury Press, Bury St Edmunds